SpringerBriefs in Education

We are delighted to announce SpringerBriefs in Education, an innovative product type that combines elements of both journals and books. Briefs present concise summaries of cutting-edge research and practical applications in education. Featuring compact volumes of 50 to 125 pages, the SpringerBriefs in Education allow authors to present their ideas and readers to absorb them with a minimal time investment. Briefs are published as part of Springer's eBook Collection. In addition, Briefs are available for individual print and electronic purchase.

SpringerBriefs in Education cover a broad range of educational fields such as: Science Education, Higher Education, Educational Psychology, Assessment & Evaluation, Language Education, Mathematics Education, Educational Technology, Medical Education and Educational Policy.

SpringerBriefs typically offer an outlet for:

- An introduction to a (sub)field in education summarizing and giving an overview of theories, issues, core concepts and/or key literature in a particular field
- A timely report of state-of-the art analytical techniques and instruments in the field of educational research
- A presentation of core educational concepts
- An overview of a testing and evaluation method
- A snapshot of a hot or emerging topic or policy change
- An in-depth case study
- A literature review
- A report/review study of a survey
- An elaborated thesis

Both solicited and unsolicited manuscripts are considered for publication in the SpringerBriefs in Education series. Potential authors are warmly invited to complete and submit the Briefs Author Proposal form. All projects will be submitted to editorial review by editorial advisors.

SpringerBriefs are characterized by expedited production schedules with the aim for publication 8 to 12 weeks after acceptance and fast, global electronic dissemination through our online platform SpringerLink. The standard concise author contracts guarantee that:

- an individual ISBN is assigned to each manuscript
- each manuscript is copyrighted in the name of the author
- the author retains the right to post the pre-publication version on his/her website or that of his/her institution

More information about this series at https://link.springer.com/bookseries/8914

Reuben Sungwa · Liz Jackson · Joyce Kahembe

Corporal Punishment in Preschool and at Home in Tanzania

A Children's Rights Challenge

 Springer

Reuben Sungwa
College of Education, Department
of Psychology and Curriculum Studies
University of Dodoma
Dodoma, Tanzania

Liz Jackson
Department of International Education
Education University of Hong Kong
Hong Kong, Hong Kong

Joyce Kahembe
Tanzania Institute of Education
Dar-es-Salaam, Tanzania

ISSN 2211-1921   ISSN 2211-193X   (electronic)
SpringerBriefs in Education
ISBN 978-981-19-1571-0   ISBN 978-981-19-1569-7   (eBook)
https://doi.org/10.1007/978-981-19-1569-7

This Springer imprint is published by the registered company Springer Nature Singapore Pte Ltd.
The registered company address is: 152 Beach Road, #21-01/04 Gateway East, Singapore 189721, Singapore

Preface

Too many children around the world face harms which they are powerless to defend themselves against without protection from others around them. As scholars, we write about this challenge primarily from an academic perspective. However, as people, we ourselves also faced and witnessed violence as children. When we were young and physically small, we were not able to stand up against corporal punishment and abuse faced by ourselves and by others around us. We therefore write this text at witnesses to violence against children in the past and present, with a commitment to prevent such harms in the future.

Despite its harmful, immoral, violent nature, injurious to individuals and to societies as a whole, corporal punishment is still used as a disciplinary tool in many homes and schools in Tanzania, and elsewhere around the world. While the practice is becoming a thing of the past in schools in many western societies, there is still widespread acceptance of its use in many contexts, including in homes in western societies, and at home and in school in much of Africa and Asia. As we discuss here, the line between corporal punishment and child abuse is unclear. That young children are abused at home by parents and corporally punished at school by teachers is commonly reported on in newspapers and other media in Tanzania, among other places. Yet in Tanzania, no serious legislative and legal actions have been taken by the government or education leaders to end these practices.

In this preface, we write from a personal perspective, to illuminate to readers why we have written this text. Through this short explanation, we invite readers to join us, not only as academics, but as persons and members of families and communities. We all can make a difference in other people's lives, including in the lives of young children. In this case, we ask you to consider the value, in the life of a community and in the life of a child, to commit to going without violence. And we ask that you do what you can to help protect the most vulnerable among us, recognizing that as a society we are only as strong and as well as our weakest link.

* * *

The primary author of this work, Reuben, was born and raised in a low-income, Christian family, in the northeastern part of Tanzania. His parents come from the largest ethnic group in Tanzania, the Sukuma people, who are well known for their conservative, traditional practices of child rearing. Among the Sukuma people, parents demand a high level of respect from their children. In this context, parents have unlimited control, and unquestionable authority over their children's life, particularly during childhood and adolescence. Sukuma parents have responsibility for nurturing, training, and raising their children. In responding to what could be interpreted as children's disrespectful behaviors, Sukuma parents use corporal punishment. In this regard, Reuben was personally subjected to corporal punishment by his parents and other adult members of his family on a regular basis throughout his childhood. His siblings and other children in the community also faced harsh corporal punishment.

Without knowing or seeing any other way, Reuben grew up believing and understanding that corporal punishment was a normal and unquestionable part of children's life. Like most children in Tanzania at that time, he did not have the opportunity to attend preschool. Before provisions for preprimary education were formalized in Tanzania in 1995, preschool education was provided only to privileged children, mainly from well-off families, or to those whose parents had exposure to preschool education. In Reuben's home district, there was only one preschool, which was run by the Mennonite Church of Tanzania. As a result of not accessing preschool education, things were not easy for Reuben upon entering school for the first time, especially in his first two years of primary school. He was frequently subjected to severe beatings from teachers when he failed to answer questions correctly or write properly. While it seemed to be suggested that these beatings would somehow "educate" on their own, Reuben was left fearful and desperate to find a way, by himself, to evade such "punishments" in the future, not learning anything more substantive from beatings. Corporal punishment was a major part of his life throughout primary and secondary school.

After he finished secondary education, Reuben joined a teachers training college, where after two years of study he graduated with a diploma in teacher education. He was then posted to work at a local ward secondary school in a remote rural village in the Dodoma Region in central Tanzania. The area was dominated by the Gogo and Hehe speaking people, who shared many characteristics of child rearing with the Sukuma. There it was also expected that children would always be respectful and show high levels of obedience to parents and other elder members of the community. And it was expected that children always abide parents' and elders' directives, without questioning. Children who did otherwise would face severe punishment.

At the school where Reuben worked, corporal punishment was common. It was used as a teaching strategy in classes and for behavior correction. Students were physically punished for such reasons as failing to pay school fees, which was hardly their personal responsibility. During that time, corporal punishment regulations from 2000 were in effect (see Chapter 3 for more). These regulations required that the head of school be the only person who administered corporal punishment to students.

However, in practice he found that this was not the case. Ordinary teachers punished students regularly without notifying the school head.

After two years, Reuben left teaching in pursuit of a Bachelor's degree in education. He majored in psychology and geography. It was during his undergraduate studies that Reuben developed an interest in early childhood education, specifically in its importance in promoting healthy physical, cognitive, emotional, social, linguistic, and spiritual development. Thereafter, he completed his Master of Arts in Education. In 2014, Reuben was awarded a scholarship to pursue his Doctor of Philosophy degree in education at the University of Hong Kong. His doctoral research conducted for his dissertation serves as the backbone to this text.

* * *

While some of the contexts and findings of this study may appear foreign to some western readers, for Liz, the second author of this text, the issues dealt with in this text remain critical around the world. Liz grew up in a poor, rural area of Oregon, United States, where she witnessed corporal punishment and child abuse at home and at school as everyday parts of life for many young children. While she herself was able to evade spankings at school, she was motivated by fear to avoid them, particularly after hearing her family and friends describe them as painful and upsetting. Less common at school, she saw that many children in her community faced abuse and neglect as well as corporal punishment at home. In relation she saw that many children, particularly from poorer families, suffered from these experiences, which effected their abilities to succeed in school and elsewhere in life, even into adulthood.

While corporal punishment became less popular in schools in the states when Liz was a child, she noticed that her community turned a blind eye to corporal punishment and child abuse at the family level, which were surrounded by privacy, shame, and silence. Parents were (are) considered above the law, as most people do not dare to intervene in another family's "private matters," despite witnessing harmful and morally wrong, abusive behavior. She saw how this impacts children, realizing that nobody took their personal protection and wellbeing in the community seriously, for themselves as growing persons, or for the development of the community. Since then, Liz has been unable to imagine any benefits to children being raised with such experiences. She observed in this context that children were effectively stigmatized and blamed, in their family and at the community level, for their innocence, vulnerability, and naivety, and sometimes for their inquisitiveness and curiosity. She still finds it shocking and disturbing that communities around the world often allow such practices, and rarely step in against unjust harm to young children.

Liz became more aware about the harms and ordinariness of school corporal punishment while working in rural South African schools in the 2000s. As with Reuben's experiences in Tanzania, she observed in South Africa young people being beaten with heavy, painful canes, for such "offenses" as arriving to school late, not knowing the answers to questions in class, and not having a proper school uniform or classroom materials (like pens and pencils). While teaching in a class, she saw her local counterparts line up entire classes of children for beatings due to apparently widespread misbehavior, or for no one answering questions correctly. While some teachers and students defended the practice and encouraged her to take part, she found that teaching was impossible when children were listening to the wails of their classmates being punished in the schoolyard. She noticed children responding with fear—physically jumping and squirming in their seats, eyes widening—as they heard repetitive screams of pain outside.

Liz did not come into the schools intending to take a stand about corporal punishment, as a white American in rural, Black South Africa. But her defiance of "cultural customs" did not go unnoticed. Soon she found herself defending her views to teachers who identified corporal punishment as mandatory, and who suggested she was interfering in the life of the school by personally refusing to take part. She was also assured it was part of the religious and cultural tradition of the community. But when some teachers described beating children as "playing policeman," she could not help but wonder whether the practice was not actually better understood as part of the legacy of Apartheid, where policemen routinely beat and abused citizens and students, to maintain a society where the majority had no rights or freedom and were systematically treated as inferior.

Some years later, while working as a professor at the University of Hong Kong, Liz was contacted by Reuben with a plan for a major study on corporal punishment in Tanzania. And she was delighted to help him gain institutional support for his research via a University of Hong Kong Postgraduate Scholarship. Reuben and Liz learned a great deal together over the years. Now Liz is honored to help support the publication of this work to give voice to ordinary people, including vulnerable children, and their right to be free from unnecessary and immoral harm, in support of the flourishing of people and their development across the lifespan within community and national contexts.

* * *

Like Reuben, Joyce grew up and was educated in Tanzania, from primary to tertiary education. Like other children in Tanzania, she faced corporal punishment for such reasons as being late to school and failing to answer questions correctly in class. She found that her teachers were not interested in listening to her views or explanations in such cases. Instead, they only judged and punished the children in their classes. Joyce also observed some of her classmates being severely punished by more than one teacher at a time, in disturbing school "parades."

In this case, Joyce often wondered quietly to herself whether corporal punishment was the best corrective measure for children. When she was very young, she often played with other children who lived on her street in Moshi Urban District in the Kilimanjaro Region. They would usually go to play far from their homes. They knew that when they came back they would be caned by their parents for wandering far away. However, she and her friends did not care very much about being caned, because they enjoyed wandering to other areas. They had become unafraid of being punished. In other words, as corporal punishment became usual to them, it did not really work as a corrective measure. On the other hand, Joyce also observed how corporal punishment could hinder learning. In secondary school, Joyce quit studying mathematics and English, although she was good in those subjects. She dropped the subjects, because her teachers would punish her whenever she made a mistake while trying to learn them.

Based on these experiences, Joyce is pleased to join Reuben and Liz to raise the voices of people, including vulnerable children; to help spread understanding that corporal punishment is unnecessary and constitutes immoral harm; and to support the use of better practices in child rearing and education.

Dodoma, Tanzania
Hong Kong, Hong Kong
Dar-es-Salaam, Tanzania

Reuben Sungwa
Liz Jackson
Joyce Kahembe

Contents

About the Authors

Reuben Sungwa is Lecturer in the Department of Educational Psychology and Curriculum Studies at the College of Education, the University of Dodoma, Tanzania. He teaches early childhood education and psychology courses in the undergraduate and graduate programs. Reuben received his Ph.D. in early childhood education at the University of Hong Kong. Prior to working in higher education, Reuben taught in secondary schools in Tanzania for over five years.

Liz Jackson is Professor and Head of the Department of International Education at the Education University of Hong Kong, and the Past President of the Philosophy of Education Society of Australasia. She is also the Former Director of the Comparative Education Research Centre at the University of Hong Kong. She worked previously in South Africa and the United Arab Emirates and has published several articles based in these contexts. She is the author of the book (with Joyce Kahembe), *Educational Assessment in Tanzania: A Sociocultural Perspective* (Springer, 2020). She is also author of the books *Questioning Allegiance: Resituating Civic Education* (Routledge, 2019) and *Beyond Virtue: The Politics of Education Emotions* (Cambridge University Press, 2020).

Joyce Kahembe is Principal Curriculum Coordinator at the Tanzania Institute of Education, which is under the Ministry of Education and Science and Technology. She previously worked at the National Examinations Council of Tanzania. She received her Ph.D. in assessment and curriculum studies at the University of Hong Kong. She is the author of the book (with Liz Jackson), *Educational Assessment in Tanzania: A Sociocultural Perspective* (Springer, 2020).

Chapter 1
Introduction

Abstract This book examines the use of corporal punishment with preschool aged children in homes and preschool settings in Tanzania. This chapter's aim is to provide a general overview of the topic and our study. First it discusses the use of corporal punishment in child rearing and in preschool education in Tanzania, as well as the views and beliefs of teachers and parents about corporal punishment and its usefulness in behavior management of children. Next, the chapter gives essential background information about education in Tanzania, as well as an explanation of the research methodology of our study. Finally, the chapter elaborates the aims of our project in relation to the global and Tanzanian challenge of corporal punishment.

Keywords Tanzania · Corporal punishment · Early childhood education · Africa · Behaviour management · Teacher perceptions · Preschool education

1.1 Introduction

In 2019, a video clip went viral on social media showing a Tanzanian regional commissioner beating a group of schoolboys (Ng'wanakilala, 2019). In the video, he is holding a stick in each hand, beating children lying on the ground, one by one. Such an act goes against Tanzanian regulations for school discipline and punishment, not to mention international conventions prohibiting corporal punishment of children. The video caught the eye of then-President of Tanzania John Magufuli. Contrary to global expectations, Magufuli had nothing but praise for the commissioner, however. As he publicly claimed in a rally shortly after the clip went viral, "I congratulated the regional commissioner for caning the students. I told him that he didn't beat them hard enough" (Ng'wanakilala, 2019).

This text explores corporal punishment in Tanzania as a historical and contemporary practice, focusing on its use with young children (six years old and younger) at home and in preschool and early childhood care facilities. Here, we take a child rights perspective on the issue. We assert that corporal punishment is not only illegal in most countries but also, more importantly, that it is an immoral practice. As spelled out in the United Nations Convention on the Rights of the Child (1990), which has been ratified by every country in the world except for the United States and

Somalia, children have inherent dignity and equal rights as young persons. Given that parents and children may have competing interests in some cases, it is the duty of parents to act in the best interest of children as vulnerable persons with evolving capacities and "weighty interests" in development, safety, social integration, and self-direction (Tillson & Oxley, 2020). In this context, corporal punishment is increasingly recognized as a barrier to education globally because it hinders child development, autonomy, and wellbeing (UNESCO, 2015). We thus contest its widespread acceptance and continued use in Tanzania (among other societies). And we interrogate here why it is that parents, caregivers, and teachers continue to use corporal punishment with young children in Tanzania, despite the emerging consensus on its harmful, immoral, and illegal nature.

In this chapter, we provide an overview about corporal punishment and our study. First, we discuss the historical controversy over corporal punishment, and its status as a child rights issue. Next, we give some essential background information about education and corporal punishment in Tanzania and explain the research methodology of the study which we report on throughout this text. Finally, we elaborate the larger aims of our project, in relation to the global and Tanzanian challenge of corporal punishment.

1.2 Research Background

Across societies, parents, caregivers, and teachers have an indispensable role in facilitating child development. They have special duties and responsibilities to socialize children, and to teach and equip them with relevant and necessary knowledge, values, and skills that will help them become a part of and interact effectively with others in society. To attain such goals, numerous child rearing and discipline styles and techniques have been and continue to be used, and they are discussed and explored by parents, academics, politicians, and other stakeholders in society at large. Amongst such techniques in child rearing is corporal punishment (CP).

CP has been a common practice in child rearing across societies in modern history. It has existed in Tanzania and many other societies for many generations (Straus, 1994). It is, in many people's minds, "as old as humankind" (Montgomery, 2009, p. 14). In school settings, CP in the past was also commonly administered around the world as a penalty to a student doing something considered wrong by the teacher, such as breaking school rules (for example, cheating on an examination, or picking fights with other students). Corporal punishment administered at home and in school can appear in many different forms, ranging from caning (beating a child with a hard cane or stick), spanking, and slapping, to requiring children to perform physically challenging tasks, such as standing on one leg for several minutes.

Defining corporal punishment is complex, however, because it has been perceived differently across time and sociocultural contexts. While there is no single universally accepted definition of corporal punishment, there is a general understanding that CP is a behavior that intends to cause pain or distress, which is administered by a more powerful person over a weaker person, as a form of punishment, discipline, or behavioral management. This definition is in line with a widely accepted definition by Straus and Donnelly (2005), which states that "corporal punishment is the use of physical force intended to cause pain, but not injury, for the purpose of correcting or controlling a child's behavior." However, many would now add to this emotionally distressing acts intended to punish, control, or correct, such as acts meant to incur embarrassment or humiliation: for example, mockery, name-calling, or requirements to do things (for example, stand on one leg) in front of others. As discussed later in this text, it can also take the form of demands by teachers or parents of children to do physically painful or harmful things, such as standing still outside in the hot sunlight for a long period of time or holding large stones high in the air.

Definitions of what CP is also intersect with attitudes and policies related to child rearing and school discipline. CP is increasingly considered a serious case of violation of children's rights and as an immoral, harmful act within the "international" (some might say western-dominated or western-influenced) community. However, it is still considered a normal and necessary aspect of child rearing in many Asian and African societies (Flynn, 1994; Gao et al., 2017; Khuwaja et al., 2018; Mwai et al., 2014; Yang, 2009). In this case, understandings about CP hinge on such factors as the way punishment is administered and the level of intensity (Baumrind, 1996; Gershoff & Bitensky, 2007). These differences can also make it difficult to estimate and compare in a standard way the prevalence of CP and common uses of CP across societies from a historical view. Different scholars (and research participants) have held divergent assumptions about what qualifies as CP, in terms of magnitude, situational appropriateness, and specific practices involved.

In many homes around the world corporal punishment is part of children's everyday lives. It is regarded by many parents and teachers as important and necessary in raising disciplined and responsible children (Durrant, 1999; Eid et al., 2018; Hecker et al., 2014; Larzelere, 2004; Mwai et al., 2014; Podana, 2018). However, during the last few decades the use of CP in child rearing and behavior modification has been subjected to increased debate (Frankenberg et al., 2010; Hecker et al., 2018; Kitano et al., 2018). Proponents of CP believe that it benefits children, and that without CP children will be uncontrollable: a menace to their own future development and to others around them (Baumrind, 1996; Boydell et al., 2017; Mararike, 2005). Other proponents argue that CP must be evaluated within a social context, as in many contexts CP is commonly judged and accepted as useful and valuable (Boydell et al., 2017; Kimani et al., 2012; Mayeza & Bhana, 2017).

In relation, corporal punishment in child rearing remains legal in many countries. In the United States, corporal punishment is legal in schools in 19 states, and at home in all states. While there are divided opinions among Americans on CP, the majority has considered it at least somewhat acceptable and appropriate in past studies (Flynn, 1994; Miller-Perrin & Perrin, 2018; Tiwari, 2019). Most American parents have also admitted to using CP on at least one occasion (Aucoin et al., 2006). Similarly, in the United Kingdom, CP also remains legal in homes, and many parents still hold positive attitudes toward it (Radford et al., 2011). And in Asian countries, CP is widely and commonly used, at homes and in schools (Chan, 2008; Chan et al., 2011; Manaay, 2013; Sanapo & Nakamura, 2011; Tang, 2006).

However, opponents of CP observe that its use is needlessly harmful and violent, while it diminishes a person's right to dignity, bodily integrity and autonomy, personal safety, and respect (Bachman et al., 2011). Despite many laypeople's sense that corporal punishment is useful and helpful to children, most studies demonstrate that beyond abstract moral and philosophical views, corporal punishment has clearly negative consequences for children (as it also has had for other groups who have been subjected to legally authorized CP in the past, such as wives, slaves, and servants; UNCRC, 2006; UNESCO, 2015). Such consequences include needless pain and distress, increased antisocial behavior, reduced self-esteem, increased levels of aggressive behavior, brain damage, depression, and bodily injuries (Gao et al., 2017; Gershoff, 2002; Hassan & Balli, 2013; Holden, 2002). Meanwhile, it encourages a culture of violence within a community, as needless pain and force against vulnerable others is encouraged within a local context and taught as if it is justified and worthwhile to the next generation. Thus, most countries in Europe have banned its use in all settings, including homes and schools (Bussmann, 2009; Gershoff, 2016).

Corporal punishment is widely supported and practiced in many societies in Africa. In most African societies, ordinary people consider CP to be important in child rearing (Boydell et al., 2017; Hecker et al., 2014; Mayeza & Bhana, 2017; Mwai et al., 2014). While all countries but one (Somalia) in Africa have ratified the United Nations Convention on the Rights of the Child (forbidding CP at home or in school settings), only seven countries out of 54 have nationally prohibited the use of CP in homes. Meanwhile, only 23 countries have explicitly banned its use in schools (Dawes et al., 2005; Global Initiative, 2012). Many African adults see CP as an appropriate means of controlling child behavior (Clacherty et al., 2005). There are various reasons given by parents and teachers to support CP. For instance, they argue that it is inexpensive, easy to administer, and always available; that it can produce an immediate response; and that little intelligence or specialized training is required for its use (Maphosa & Shumba, 2010).

Although Tanzania is a signatory to the Convention on the Rights of the Child, CP is still used and widely regarded as legal across the country (Feinstein & Mwahombela, 2010; Frankenberg et al., 2010; Hecker et al., 2018; Kuleana, 1997). While many in Tanzania today describe CP as an important part of traditional African culture and their religious values (particularly relating it to their Christian or Islamic teachings), the institutionalization of corporal punishment in Tanzania can be more specifically traced back to the legacy of the German and British colonial administrations and goes beyond (and indeed actually contradicts) biblical and other religious teachings. The colonial period in Tanzania (and elsewhere) was characterized by the formal sanctioning and widespread caning (and other punishments) not only of local children, but also of local adults who disobeyed colonial orders (Mwakikagile, 2000). In this context of widespread colonial oppression of local people, in Tanzania and throughout much of Africa, practices of institutionalized violence by those with questionable authority and influence were gradually accepted and then supported by native Tanzanians. CP thus became more broadly integrated over time into local practices of child rearing and education.

An earlier cross-sectional study conducted in southern Tanzania revealed that 95% of primary school-aged children experienced corporal punishment both at school and at home (Hecker et al., 2014). Most parents and teachers in Tanzania defend it as an appropriate method of controlling child behavior; some even describe it as an expression of love for children (Feinstein & Mwahombela, 2010; Furnham, 2005). Nonetheless, in Tanzanian schools (as elsewhere) CP has been identified as one reason for truancy and drop out, in addition to the development of significant personal and social problems (Feinstein & Mwahombela, 2010; Tanzania Institute of Education, 2021). Thus, the limited research on corporal punishment in Tanzania echoes findings from other societies related to the harms it incurs in relation to child dignity, welfare, and future self-direction and positive autonomy.

However, no study has examined the use of corporal punishment with young children (6 years old and younger) in Tanzania. The paucity of information here hinders efforts to understand challenges children in the society face and to protect children from harm. In the long run, this situation negatively impacts child development and school learning, and harms society more generally in terms of equality, human rights, positive relationships, community wellbeing, and social and educational development.

This book reports on our study to more holistically understand the situation of CP with young children in families and in preschool settings in Tanzania, against the broader backdrop of child rights and other important social and cultural considerations. Specifically, our study focuses on identifying parents, educators, and educational policy makers' experiences and views related to using CP with young children in homes and preschools. Additionally, our study explores the perceptions of parents, teachers, and educational policy makers toward legal instruments and possibilities to restrict and eliminate the practice in Tanzania in the future. Our study thus adds valuable findings to illuminate a serious situation that has not yet received due attention. And it highlights what can and should be done to protect young children in Tanzania from the harms and risks caused by corporal punishment in the future.

1.3 Our Study

The general objective of our study is to improve education and childcare in preschool and family settings through developing a better understanding of how and why corporal punishment is used by parents, teachers, and other caregivers with young children (aged six years and younger) in Tanzania. Specifically, we aimed to:

1. Explore parents and educators' attitudes toward CP in homes and preschool settings,
2. Identify factors influencing parents and preschool teachers' use of CP with young children, and

3. Analyze the efficacy of existing policies, laws, and regulations on child protection and CP in Tanzania.

Our study primarily takes a qualitative approach, to gain understanding of people's views and conceptions of the matter at hand (Denzin & Lincoln, 1994; Stake, 1995). In our study, we employ a single case study design with embedded cases (Creswell, 2007; Stake, 1995). This enables us to explore and understand in a detailed manner the complexity of the phenomenon and reflect deeply on diverse participants' views. However, some elements of a quantitative approach were also incorporated for roughly estimating the prevalence of corporal punishment use with young children in our study context. Additionally, we rely on philosophical analysis and argumentation to provide moral arguments regarding the harmfulness and wrongness of corporal punishment across societies, including Tanzania.

1.3.1 Research Context and Case Selection

Our study is conducted in Tanzania. Contemporary Tanzania is a historical union of the mainland territory/state of Tanganyika, and the adjacent island of Zanzibar. Tanganyika, formerly a German and then a British colony, regained independence in 1961. Zanzibar, which has its own distinctive colonial and cultural history (and is currently a semi-autonomous region of Tanzania), obtained its independence from the British in 1964. To the south, Tanzania shares borders with Malawi, Mozambique, and Zambia; to the north are Kenya and Uganda; and to the west are Burundi, Rwanda, and the Democratic Republic of Congo. To its east is the Indian Ocean. Tanzania has a young, dependent population. About 44% of the population are children below the age of 14 (National Bureau of Statistics [NBS], 2012). Life expectancy in Tanzania is 62 years for males and 64 years for females, and the literacy rate is 72% (NBS, 2014).

Past studies of corporal punishment in Tanzania were conducted in Dar es Salaam, Mara, Mbeya, Iringa, and Arusha (Frankenberg et al., 2010; Hecker et al., 2014; Kuleana, 1997; Yaghambe & Tshabangu, 2013). Our study is conducted in the Dodoma Urban District (Dodoma Municipal Council) in Dodoma Region. Dodoma is the capital of Tanzania, a centrally positioned region with more than two million people (NBS, 2012). While this region (particularly the urban district) has experienced rapid development, most people there still live essentially from agriculture and livestock keeping. Meanwhile, the remote parts of the region remain the poorest and driest in the country, suffering frequent famines (White-Kaba et al., 2011).

The native inhabitants of Dodoma Region are Gogo and Rangi-speaking people. However, the Dodoma Urban District's development has attracted people from all corners of the country. It is now inhabited by people from many different tribes and backgrounds, making it one of the richest districts in terms of cultural, economic, and linguistic diversity. The district is also among the top districts for the number of children enrolled in preschool. According to Basic Education Statistics of Tanzania (BEST, 2018), 68,840 children were enrolled in preschools in the region in 2018.

In the urban district, 12,470 children were enrolled in preschool: 9,009 children in public preschools and 3,461 in private preschools (BEST, 2018).

Participants for our study were drawn from the Kizota ward within the Dodoma Urban District. The Kizota ward is located at the center of the district. It is the oldest and most populous among the 37 wards in the district, with a population of over 34,453 (NBS, 2012). In 2018 (BEST), 1,237 children were enrolled in preschools in the ward. Kizota ward has 8 public preschools, all attached to primary schools, and 6 private preschools. In Tanzania, families with higher socioeconomic backgrounds normally enroll their children in private schools, where the standard of education is higher. Thus, one public preschool and one private preschool were selected randomly to participate in our study. In addition, one international private preschool was selected.

1.3.2 Data Collection

Within each site, we employed survey questionnaires, semi-structured interviews, and observations to collect data from parents and teachers (including heads of school). We also conducted interviews with district and regional educational policy makers. Self-administered questionnaires helped obtain information about participants' attitudes toward using corporal punishment with preschool-aged children and their understanding of relevant child protection policies and laws. Due to the nature of this study and its unique social-cultural setting, we adapted questionnaires used in previous studies (El-Makzoum, 2015; Hunter et al., 2000; Manaay, 2013; Nashmi, 2008; Youssef et al., 1998). Questionnaires for teachers were distributed and collected by the lead researcher (Reuben) personally, to ensure confidentiality and maximize the response rate. Questionnaires were sent to parents by their children. Questionnaires were sent to all participants during early to mid-2016. As discussed below, a minority of participants did not return questionnaires by the end of our data collection period; they were considered unwilling to participate in our study.

Through interviews, we collected additional, more in-depth information about participants' views and understandings. A predetermined set of questions was prepared to guide interviews with parents, preschool teachers, heads of school, and educational policy makers. Teachers were selected for interviews based on their willingness to participate as indicated in their responses to the questionnaire. Likewise, parents' responses to the questionnaire and other criteria, such as number of children, level of education, financial status, age, and marital status, were used to select parents for interviews. Parents were particularly recruited from low-income, middle-income, and high-income families. With the aid of research assistants, we also recruited 3 parents of young out-of-school children to participate in interviews.

Interviews were conducted from mid to late-2016. Each participant was interviewed individually in a calm environment, with each interview taking 35 to 50 min. Every participant was provided the opportunity to decide the time, location, and date of their interview. In this regard, all teachers preferred for their interview to be conducted at school, while interviews with parents were conducted at their homes. The lead researcher (Reuben) visited the homes of parents before the interviews took place, to build rapport and gain a better understanding of their home environment and living conditions. Interviews with educational policy makers were conducted at various locations. Interviews were generally conducted in Kiswahili, the common spoken language in Tanzania. Interviews were audio recorded while notes were taken, with advance permission gained from participants. Pseudonyms are used here to maintain confidentiality.

Observations were also conducted in each of the preschools, with teachers who indicated their willingness to participate. Before observations, the lead researcher visited the site for the purpose of establishing his general trustworthiness. In each preschool, Reuben observed classroom and school activities, like play, meals, class size, and class arrangements. For observation, Reuben prepared and used guides to systematically observe teacher-student relationships and interactions, student–student relationships, teacher-student ratios, and teacher-teacher interactions. There was also a focus on how the teachers managed discipline and punishment. During observations, Reuben took pictures of different aspects of the schools and classrooms to better remember the settings and the events and activities that transpired.

Most of the primary data collection was conducted by Reuben. However, we also employed two research assistants with familiarity with the location and the ability to understand and speak Gogo and Rangi, the two languages commonly spoken by local people. These research assistants helped minimize the potential problem of language barriers with relevant stakeholders not conversant in Kiswahili. Moreover, the inclusion of assistants in data collection, analysis, and interpretation provided a more balanced account through triangulation of perspectives. In relation, we used back translation to enhance validity of data. In this regard, interview schedules first prepared in English were translated into Kiswahili to ease communication with participants. The research team also translated them into Gogo or Rangi for some interviews. Then we transcribed interviews verbatim and translated each into English from Gogo, Rangi, or Kiswahili. Some interviews were then selected for back translation to the original text, to verify the accuracy of translation. In terms of recruitment, participation, and use of human data, this study followed all research ethical guidelines as stipulated by the University of Hong Kong.

1.3.3 Participants

The lead researcher (Reuben) distributed self-administered questionnaires to 28 teachers: at least 9 teachers at each school, selected at random. However, 7 (25%) teachers did not return their questionnaires. In addition, one teacher from each preschool was recruited for class observation and interview, and one head from each school was interviewed. Therefore, this study involved a total of 24 teachers: 3 heads of school and 21 regular classroom teachers. Although we aimed to have gender balance, men are significantly underrepresented in preschool education in Tanzania. Among teachers, 18 (75%) were female, and 6 (25%) were male. The majority of teachers (46%) who participated held a grade "A" teaching certificate. This is the minimum level of qualification to perform teaching activities in Tanzania. Nine (38%) held higher diploma degrees, and four (17%) were university graduates. 67% identified as Christian, and 21% as Muslim. 12% did not disclose their religious identity.

Participating teachers varied in age. The youngest was 23, and the oldest was 65 at the time of data collection. Their years of teaching experience varied from 2 to 36. Most (63%) joined the teaching profession after 2000. This is relevant, because in 2000 the government of Tanzania amended the CP regulations of 1979. With the new amendment (as will be discussed later), only the head of the school is legally allowed to administer corporal punishment to students. Hence, it is presumed that most of these teachers began teaching in the period when corporal punishment was more likely to be monitored and controlled, although it was still basically legal in schools. Table 1.1 provides a summary of this demographic information.

29 parents participated in this study: 26 parents with children in preschool, and 3 parents of children who were not in preschool. Enrollment in preschools in Tanzania is not mandatory, but it is free in public preschools for children between 5 to 6 years old. However, in 2013, the rate of access to preschool in the Dodoma Urban District was only 43% (BEST, 2013). In this context, we wanted to also learn from parents of children who were not attending preschool, to obtain a broader picture of CP with young children in the region. For those attending preschool, questionnaires were distributed to 30 parents via their children. 10 parents were selected at random from each preschool. Out of 30 surveys distributed, 26 were returned. Based on their responses to the questionnaires, 3 parents of children in preschool, one from each school, were selected for interviews. With the aid of research assistants, we also recruited 3 parents of out-of-school young children in the district to participate in interviews.

Parents who participated in our study had been residents of the Dodoma Urban District for at least ten years. 76% of participating parents were mothers and 24% were fathers. As indicated in Table 1.2, at the time of data collection, 24 (83%) parents were married, 4 (14%) were not married, and one (3%) was widowed. Mothers were aged 27 to 54 years old, while fathers were aged 24 to 45 years old. Almost half of parents (15) had 4 to 6 children. The majority (69%) were Christian, 24% were Muslims, and 7% did not disclose their religious identity. Among fathers, four were government employees, one was a politician, and one was in business. Nine mothers were employed, five were housewives, and eight were in business.

We also recruited five educational policy makers to provide information by way of interviews about policy and legal issues related to child rights and corporal punishment in the country and district. The educational policy makers were recruited from the District Education Office, the District School Inspectorate (Quality Control), and the Regional Education Office. These participants were purposively selected by virtue of their official capacity. They represented a group responsible for developing education district and/or regional-level policies and circulars to guide activities and

Table 1.1 Demographic information for teachers

	Sex	Marital status	Age	Number of children	Religion	Years of experience	Education	Role
1	F	Married	54	5	Christian	26	B. A	Head
2	F	Married	50	4	Christian	21	Diploma	Head
3	M	Married	48	5	Christian	18	Diploma	Head
4	F	Married	30	2	Christian	5	Certificate	Teacher
5	F	Married	42	3	Christian	14	Diploma	Teacher
6	F	Unknown	28	1	Christian	4	Diploma	Teacher
7	F	Single	26	0	Christian	2	Certificate	Teacher
8	F	Single	23	0	Christian	2	Certificate	Teacher
9	F	Married	38	4	Muslim	11	B. A	Teacher
10	F	Married	47	5	Unknown	20	Certificate	Teacher
11	F	Married	33	3	Christian	5	Diploma	Teacher
12	M	Single	30	1	Unknown	6	Certificate	Teacher
13	F	Single	25	1	Christian	2	Diploma	Teacher
14	F	Single	28	2	Christian	4	Certificate	Teacher
15	F	Married	29	3	Christian	3	B. A	Teacher
16	F	Single	24	0	Christian	2	Diploma	Teacher
17	F	Married	47	4	Muslim	21	Certificate	Teacher
18	F	Married	48	3	Muslim	19	Certificate	Teacher
19	M	Unknown	33	2	Christian	7	Diploma	Teacher
20	F	Single	30	1	Christian	3	Diploma	Teacher
21	M	Married	44	4	Muslim	20	Certificate	Teacher
22	M	Married	65	6	Unknown	36	B. A	Teacher
23	F	Married	49	5	Christian	23	Certificate	Teacher
24	M	Single	24	0	Muslim	2	Certificate	Teacher

administration of school education. We assumed (correctly) that this group would be much more knowledgeable about educational policies, procedures, laws, rules, and regulations in Tanzania, and the sanctioned use of CP than our other study participants. Table 1.3 presents demographic information about the participating educational policy makers. 4 were male, and one was female. They were all Christian, aged 36 to 52 years old. All were university graduates. 3 of them held a master's degree in education management and policy, and one was also enrolled in a master's degree program at the time of the study.

Table 1.2 Demographic information for parents

	Sex	Marital status	Age	Number of children	Religion	Level of education	Occupation
1	F	Married	48	6	Christian	Diploma	Accountant
2	F	Married	33	3	Christian	Primary	Housewife
3	F	Married	42	5	Muslim	University	Civil servant
4	F	Married	31	4	Christian	Secondary	Business
5	F	Married	50	3	Christian	Primary	Housewife
6	M	Married	37	4	Unknown	Secondary	Politician
7	F	Married	41	2	Christian	Primary	Housewife
8	M	Single	26	1	Christian	Secondary	Civil servant
9	F	Married	29	3	Muslim	Secondary	Secretary
10	F	Single	27	1	Christian	Diploma	Librarian
11	M	Married	30	2	Christian	University	Police officer
12	F	Married	36	4	Christian	Primary	Business
13	F	Married	31	3	Unknown	Diploma	Social worker
14	F	Widowed	54	6	Christian	Primary	Business
15	M	Married	45	4	Christian	University	Magistrate
16	M	Single	24	1	Christian	Secondary	Civil servant
17	F	Married	29	3	Muslim	Diploma	Civil servant
18	F	Married	36	3	Muslim	Primary	Housewife
19	F	Married	40	5	Christian	Primary	Business
20	F	Married	25	2	Christian	Primary	Housewife
21	M	Married	44	6	Christian	U/degree	Business
22	F	Married	38	4	Muslim	Primary	Business
23	F	Married	51	6	Christian	U/degree	Doctor
24	F	Married	46	5	Christian	Primary	Business
25	F	Single	30	1	Christian	Secondary	Nurse
26	F	Married	41	5	Muslim	Primary	Social worker
27	F	Married	43	5	Christian	Primary	Business
28	M	Married	37	4	Christian	Secondary	Priest
29	F	Married	45	3	Muslim	Primary	Business

1.3.4 Pilot Study

Prior to the main study, a pilot study was conducted at two other randomly selected preschools in the Dodoma Urban District. The pilot study helped uncover ethical and technological problems that were likely to impact findings: for example, problems related to the use and positioning of recording instruments, access to research sites, and the establishment of relationships with participants. For the pilot, we distributed

Table 1.3 Demographic information about educational policy makers

	Sex	Marital status	Age	Number of children	Religion	Years of experience	Education
1	M	Married	49	4	Christian	21	M. A
2	M	Married	52	3	Christian	24	M. A
3	M	Married	38	2	Christian	11	M. A
4	F	Married	36	2	Christian	5	B. A
5	M	Married	45	4	Christian	15	B. A

questionnaires to 10 teachers and 18 parents associated with the selected preschools. The lead researcher (Reuben) also conducted interviews with 2 teachers, 4 parents, and 2 heads of school. Also, the lead researcher observed 2 lessons: one at each school.

The pilot study intended not only to examine the appropriateness of interview and survey questions and the duration of interviews, but also to evaluate whether they would gather useful data (Denzin & Lincoln, 1994). As a result, some interview and survey questions were refined or reworded to avoid ambiguity and ease understanding. Some questions were deleted because they appeared repetitive. In addition, in the final study, the time for returning questionnaires was extended from one to two weeks. This was important to give enough time for participants to respond to questionnaires and increase the rate of return. Following the pilot, some changes were also made with regard to study participants. In the main study, two further categories were added: parents of out-of-preschool children, and educational policy makers.

Furthermore, the pilot study helped the lead researcher (Reuben) to understand his position and role as a researcher within the social context. For example, he found that more informal interactions during recruitment and data gathering were more productive than formal interactions. During interviews, participants responded more freely when Reuben behaved more informally. In addition, after the pilot study research assistants fluent in Gogo and Rangi were employed to assist in data collection where participants were not fully comfortable with Kiswahili or English.

1.4 Significance of Our Study

Our study provides new insights and understanding about parents and preschool teachers' support of CP in early childhood care and education in Tanzania, despite its harmfulness to children and communities. As such, it can help policy makers and other stakeholders, including teachers and parents, to develop more effective and sustainable childcare and educational approaches that can better enhance children's positive moral and emotional development. Moreover, the findings of this study can be useful to educational authorities and teacher trainers when designing teacher education curriculum that focuses on student discipline. In relation, our study confirms, clarifies, and extends findings from many others, illustrating that teacher education related to student discipline is insufficient in Tanzania today (Yaghambe & Tshabangu, 2013). In parallel, the findings contribute to a better understanding of the need for Tanzanian parents to be educated about childcare and discipline practices beyond CP, to encourage alternative, more positive forms of behavior management and punishment. Finally, our study has legal implications, as it indicates and helps explain the inefficacy of current rules, policy, and regulations at the international and national levels to decrease or eliminate corporal punishment in schools and homes in Tanzania.

1.5 Book Outline

The purpose of this chapter was to provide background information about the problem informing our research, and the nature of the study we are reporting on here. The next chapter reviews the global literature related to corporal punishment. The chapter begins with a description of the importance of care for young children and preschool education, before discussing corporal punishment and conflicting perspectives on its use. In addition, the chapter summarizes past research literature that traces the major factors that influence the use of corporal punishment of children across societies. Finally, the chapter explores global legal and constitutional frameworks for child rights protection and highlights the importance of banning corporal punishment as a moral and social imperative, going beyond matters of legality.

Chapter 3 describes the historical background and recent research on attitudes toward the use of corporal punishment in homes and preschool settings in Tanzania. It also analyses the legal framework which currently permits corporal punishment in Tanzanian homes and schools, despite Tanzania's ratification of the United Nations Convention on the Right of the Child (which emphatically forbids CP at home and in school). Chapter 4 focuses on the findings of our study, sharing in detail the views and attitudes of teachers, parents, and educational policy makers about CP, and our analysis of the factors influencing the use of corporal punishment by parents and teachers, based on our data. Chapter 5 provides the conclusion to the book, including recommendations for further research and for future practice related to our study.

References

Aucoin, K., Frick, P., & Bodin, S. (2006). Corporal punishment and child adjustment. *Journal of Applied Developmental Psychology, 27*(6), 527–541.

Bachman, R., Randolph, A., & Brown, B. L. (2011). Predicting perceptions of fear at school and going to and from school for African-American and White students: The effects of school security measures. *Youth & Society, 43*(2), 705–726.

Basic Education Statistics in Tanzania (BEST). (2013). *Basic education statistics in Tanzania: National data 2009–2013*. Ministry of Education and Vocational Training.

Basic Education Statistics in Tanzania (BEST). (2014). *Basic education statistics in Tanzania: National data 2010–2014*. Ministry of Education and Vocational Training.

Basic Education Statistics in Tanzania (BEST). (2018). *Basic education statistics in Tanzania: National data 2017–2018*. Ministry of Education and Vocational Training.

Baumrind, D. (1996). The discipline controversy revisited. *Family Relations, 45*, 405–415.

Boydell, N., Nalukenge, W., Siu, G., Seeley, J., & Wight, D. (2017). How mothers in poverty explain their use of corporal punishment: A qualitative study in Kampala, Uganda. *The European Journal of Development Research, 29*(5), 999–1016.

Bussmann, K. D. (2009). *The effect of banning corporal punishment in Europe: A five-nation comparison*. Martin-Luther-University.

Chan, K. L. (2008). *Study on child-friendly families: Immunity from domestic violence*. University of Hong Kong.

Chan, Y. C., Lam, G. L. T., & Shae, W. C. (2011). Children's views on child abuse and neglect: Findings from an exploratory study with Chinese children in Hong Kong. *Child Abuse & Neglect, 35*, 162–172.

Clacherty, G., Donald, D., & Clacherty, A. (2005). *South African children's experiences of corporal punishment*. Save the Children Sweden.

Creswell, J. W. (2007). *Qualitative inquiry and research design: Choosing among five approaches*. Sage.

Dawes, A., Kropiwnicki, Z., Kafaar, Z., & Richter, L. (2005). *Corporal punishment of children: A South African national survey*. Human Science Research Council.

Denzin, N., & Lincoln, Y. (1994). *Handbook of qualitative research*. Sage.

Durrant, J. E. (1999). Evaluating the success of Sweden's corporal punishment ban. *Child Abuse and Neglect, 23*, 435–448.

Eid, B., Touma, B., Marianne, L., Khabbaz, R., & Gerbaka, B. (2018). Corporal punishment of children: Discipline or abuse? *Libyan Journal of Medicine, 13*(1), 1485456.

El-Makzoum, H. (2015). *Understanding physical punishment as a method of disciplining children in Libya: The perspectives of parents, children and professionals* (Unpublished PhD Thesis). University of Sheffield.

Feinstein, S., & Mwahombela, L. (2010). Corporal punishment in Tanzania's schools. *International Review of Education, 56*, 399–410.

Flynn, C. P. (1994). Regional differences in attitudes towards corporal punishment. *Journal of Marriage and the Family, 56*, 314–324.

Frankenberg, S. J., Holmqvist, R., & Rubenson, B. (2010). The care of corporal punishment: Conceptions of early childhood discipline strategies among parents and grandparents in a poor and urban area in Tanzania. *Childhood, 17*(4), 455–469.

Furnham, A. (2005). Lay theories of corporal punishment. In M. Donnelly, & M. A. Straus (Eds.), *Corporal punishment of children in theoretical perspective*. Yale University Press.

Gao, Y., Atkinson, S., & Xing, L. (2017). Prevalence and risk factors of child maltreatment among migrant families in China. *Child Abuse & Neglect, 65*, 171–181.

Gershoff, E. T. (2002). Corporal punishment by parents and associated child behaviors and experiences: A meta-analytic and theoretical review. *Psychological Bulletin, 128*, 539–579.

Gershoff, E. T. (2016). Should parents' physical punishment of children be considered a source of toxic stress that affects brain development? *Family Relations, 65*, 151–162.

Gershoff, E. T., & Bitensky, S. H. (2007). The case against corporal punishment of children: Converging evidence from social science research and international human rights law and implications for U.S. public policy. *Psychology, Public Policy, and Law, 13*(4), 231–272.

Global Initiative to End All Corporal Punishment of Children. (2012). *United Republic of Tanzania: Country report*. End Violence Against Children.

Hassan, A. H., & Balli, T. A. L. (2013). Assessing the effects of corporal punishment on primary school pupils' academic performance and discipline in Unguja, Zanzibar. *International Journal of Education and Research, 1*(12), 1–12.

Hecker, T., Goessmann, K., Nkuba, M., & Hermenau, K. (2018). Teachers' stress intensifies violent disciplining in Tanzanian secondary schools. *Child Abuse & Neglect, 76*, 173–183.

Hecker, T., Hermenau, K., Isele, D., & Elbert, T. (2014). Corporal punishment and children's externalizing problems: A cross sectional study of Tanzanian primary school aged children. *Child Abuse & Neglect, 38*, 884–892.

Holden, G. W. (2002). Perspectives on the effects of corporal punishment: Comment on Gershoff (2002). *Psychological Bulletin, 128*, 590–595.

Hunter, W., Jain, D., Sadowski, L., & Sanhueza, A. (2000). Risk factors for severe child discipline practices in rural India. *Journal of Pediatric Psychology, 25*(6), 435–447.

Kaltenbach, E., Hermenau, K., Nkuba, M., Goessmann, K., & Hecker, T. (2018). Interaction competencies with children: A prevention training to reduce corporal punishment by teachers. *Journal of Aggression, Maltreatment and Trauma, 27*(1), 35–53.

Khuwaja, H., Karmaliani, R., McFarlane, J., Somani, R., Gulzar, S., & Ali, T. S. (2018). The intersection of school corporal punishment and associated factors: Baseline results from a randomized controlled trial in Pakistan. *PLoS ONE, 13*(10), 20–30.

Kimani, G. N., Kara, K. M., & Ogetange, T. B. (2012). Teachers and pupils' views on persistent use of corporal punishment in managing discipline in primary schools in Starehe division, Kenya. *International Journal of Humanities and Social Science, 2*(19), 268–274.

Kitano, N., Yoshimasu, K., Yamamoto, B. A., & Nakamura, Y. (2018). Associations between childhood experiences of parental corporal punishment and neglectful parenting and undergraduate students' endorsement of corporal punishment as an acceptable parenting strategy. *PLoS ONE, 13*(10), 206–243.

Kuleana. (1997). *Study on corporal punishment in primary schools in Mara region.* Kuleana Centre for Children's Rights.

Kuleana. (1999). *The state of education in Tanzania.* Kuleana Centre for Children's Rights.

Larzelere, R. E. (2004). *Sweden's smacking ban: More harm than good.* Families First and The Christian Institute.

Manaay, S. M. (2013). *Discipline in the Philippine context: Factors affecting parents' use of corporal punishment* (Unpublished PhD Thesis). The Chicago School of Professional Psychology

Maphosa, C., & Shumba, A. (2010). Educators' disciplinary capabilities after the banning of corporal punishment in South African schools. *South African Journal of Education, 30*, 387–399.

Mararike, C. (2005). *Spare the rod, save the child.* IRIN.

Mayeza, E., & Bhana, D. (2017). Addressing gender violence among children in the early years of schooling: Insights from teachers in a South African primary school. *International Studies in Sociology of Education, 26*(4), 408–425.

Miles, M. B., & Hubberman, A. M. (1994). *Qualitative data analysis.* SAGE.

Miller-Perrin, C., & Perrin, R. (2018). Physical punishment of children by US parents: Moving beyond debate to promote children's health and wellbeing. *Psicologia: Reflexão e Crítica, 31*, 16.

Montgomery, H. (2009). *An introduction to childhood: Anthropological perspectives on children's lives.* Willey-Blackwell.

Mwai, B. K., Kimengi, I. N., & Kipsoi, E. J. (2014). Perceptions of teachers on the ban of corporal punishment in pre-primary institutions in Kenya. *World Journal of Education, 4*(6), 90–100.

Mwakikagile, G. (2000). *Africa and the West.* Nova.

Nashmi, A. (2008). *The use of physical punishment on children in Saudi Arabia. Perceptions and experiences of parents and young people* (Unpublished PhD Thesis). Durham University.

National Bureau of Statistics (NBS). (2012). *Tanzania national population census report.* Government Press.

National Bureau of Statistics (NBS). (2014). *Tanzania basic demographic and socio-economic profile.* Government press.

Ng'wanakilala, F. (2019, October 5). Tanzanian president backs official who beat students with a stick. *Reuters.*

Podana, Z. (2018). Corporal punishment of children by parents in the Czech Republic: Attitudes, prevalence rates, and intergenerational transmission of violence. *Auc Philosophica Et Historica, 2*, 57–76.

Radford, L., Corral, S., Bradley, C., Fisher, H., Bassett, C., Howat, N., & Collishaw, S. (2011). *Child abuse and neglect in the UK today*. National Society for the Prevention of Cruelty to Children.

Sanapo, M. S., & Nakamura, Y. (2011). Gender and physical punishment: The Filipino children's experience. *Child Abuse Review, 20*, 39–56.

Stake, R. E. (1995). *The art of case study research: Perspectives on practice*. Sage.

Straus, M. A. (1994). *Beating the devil out of them: Corporal punishment in American families*. Lexington.

Straus, M. A., & Donnelly, D. (2005). *Corporal punishment of children in theoretical perspective*. Yale University Press.

The Tanzania Institute of Education & UNESCO. (2021). *Connect with respect: Curriculum for improving learning environment through building skills for respectful and non-violent relationship in Tanzanian schools*. Tanzania Institute of Education.

Tang, C. S. (2006). Corporal punishment and physical maltreatment against children: A community study on Chinese parents in Hong Kong. *Child Abuse & Neglect, 30*, 893–907.

Tiwari, A. (2019). The corporal punishment ban in schools: Teachers' attitudes and classroom practices. *Educational Studies, 45*(3), 271–284).

Tillson, J., & Oxley, L. (2020). Children's moral rights and UK school exclusions. *Theory and Research in Education*, published online first.

United Nations Commission on Human Rights. (1990). *Conventions on the rights of the child*. United Nations.

United Nations Convention on the Rights of the Child (UNCRC). (2006). *General comment No. 8*. United Nations.

UNESCO. (2015). *School-related gender-based violence is preventing the achievement of quality education for all*. UNESCO.

The United Republic of Tanzania (URT). (1995). *Education, training and policy*. Government Press.

White-Kaba, A. A., Andrea, K., & Shao, C. (2011). *Changing gender dynamics through community-based health initiatives, Dodoma region, Tanzania*. Dodoma: CBHI.

Yaghambe, R. S., & Tshabangu, I. (2013). Disciplinary networks in secondary schools: Policy dimensions and children's rights in Tanzania. *Journal of Studies in Education, 3*(4), 42–56.

Yang, S. (2009). Cane of love: Parental attitudes towards corporal punishment in Korea. *British Journal of Social Work, 39*, 1540–1555.

Youssef, R. M., Attia, M. S., & Kamel, M. I. (1998). Children experiencing violence: Prevalence and determinants of corporal punishment in schools. *Child Abuse & Neglect, 22*(10), 975–985.

Chapter 2
Corporal Punishment: Global Perspectives

Abstract This chapter reviews research and legal perspectives on early child development and corporal punishment from a global view. The chapter begins with a description of the importance of preschool education and early childhood care, and then analyzes conflicting perspectives on the use of corporal punishment generally and with preschool-aged children. Next, research on the prevalence of corporal punishment and attitudes about it across diverse societies is presented. Finally, the chapter discusses the international legal framework to protect children from corporal punishment and other forms of violence, particularly the United Nations Convention on Rights of the Child of 1990 and the African Charter on the Rights and Welfare of the Child of 2003, and articulates moral and religious arguments against the use of corporal punishment. Thus, this chapter argues against corporal punishment, generally and with young (preschool-aged) children, in light of its serious harms to children and negative repercussions for society.

Keywords Tanzania · Corporal punishment · Child development · Early childhood education · Policy analysis · Children's rights · Child welfare

2.1 The Importance of Early Child Development

Physically and emotionally, early childhood care and education is of the utmost importance to children's (human's) lives. A good start in life has an everlasting impact on personal economic and sociocultural development (Elliott, 2006; Heckman & Masterov, 2004; Naudeau, 2011). Early childhood care and education form the basis for future, lifelong development, and for gaining a sense of emotional security and wellbeing. Thus, early childhood is the most significant stage in the holistic process of child development and school learning (Pudaruth & Bahadoor, 2011).

From a neurological perspective, brain development is most rapid in the first three years of life. This is a critical period for a child's future learning and proper functioning as an adult, during which stimulation from the environment is essential (Shonkoff & Phillips, 2000). During these early years, a supportive environment ensured by immediate care providers, family members, and other people around the child is essential to help them build a sense of self-control and self-efficacy, while a less positive environment can negatively affect cognitive, emotional, and social development.

In this context, preschool education lays an important foundation for present and later learning (Heckman & Masterov, 2004; Naudeau, 2011; UNESCO, 2011). In research, preschool education is associated with increased employment opportunities later in life, due to various social and academic skills that a child can acquire and develop during this period (Heckman, 2010; Naudeau, 2011). Preschool education is important for all children. In developing countries, participation in preschool is strongly correlated with increases in girls' enrollment in and completion of later levels of schooling (Heckman, 2010; UNESCO, 2007, 2010). Given the significance of early childhood development and preschool education in the human lifespan, the prevalence of corporal punishment in childcare and in the education of young children is of considerable importance. More specifically, the continued use of corporal punishment with young children despite its harmfulness (to children and communities) is an urgent issue.

2.2 Conflicting Perspectives on Corporal Punishment

2.2.1 Definitions and Debates

As briefly discussed in the last chapter, corporal punishment (CP) is understood and employed somewhat differently across societies around the world. In general, it is commonly defined as the "use of physical force intended to cause pain or discomfort, however light, but not injury, for the purpose of correcting or controlling a child's behavior" (Straus & Donnelly, 2005). According to UNICEF (2010), CP is "is the use of physical force intending to cause pain, but not wounds, as a means of discipline." Another definition is "behaviors, which do not result in significant physical injury, such as spanking and slapping, whereas behaviors such as punching, hitting, beating, kicking, burning which results into injury are considered as physical abuse" (Gershoff, 2002). These definitions provide two key features of CP. First, it is a deliberate action, and second, it is meant to cause some pain or discomfort, but not "serious" or "severe" injury.

These definitions suggest that corporal punishment is understood as different from abuse, which is associated with more serious harm. However, child abuse, like CP, is conceptualized differently across sociocultural contexts, while professionals in the field do not always agree on its constitutive features in detail. Meadow (1993) defines child abuse as an improper way of treating a child that is incompatible with the existing norms and standards of a society. On the other hand, the World Health Organization (WHO) views child abuse as comprising all types of "physical, emotional, sexual abuse and neglect or negligent treatment" which could lead to "actual or possible damage to the child's health, survival, development or dignity" (2005). More generally, abuse can be defined as "non-accidental action by parents, teachers, caregivers or any other authoritative figure that results in a child being hurt or injured" (Straus, 2010). Significantly, however, many incidences of abuse start as CP, with the desire to instill discipline rather than to engage in harmful abuse (Gershoff, 2002).

Abuse can be physical as well as sexual, and all forms of abuse entail emotionally abusive impacts (Straus, 2010). People who are abused or otherwise harmed by others are likely to feel uncared for, neglected, despised, weak, insecure, and disempowered. In relation, recent definitions of corporal punishment also include a focus on punishments that are intended to bring about emotional and psychological distress and discomfort. This may include such acts as name calling, scolding, mocking, or forcing children to engage in uncomfortable or painful, embarrassing, or disturbing activities. Such behaviors are increasingly considered abusive, unnecessary, and unhelpful, whether employed with adults or children. Such behaviors have also been seen to have long-term negative psychological, emotional, and cognitive impacts, although they remain widely used in many contexts in child rearing and education.

CP divides people across and within societies (Ripoll-Nunez & Rohner, 2006). Though many feel that using CP in a systematic and deliberate way is effective for modifying behavior (Domjan, 2000), studies show that in most cases it has negative impacts on child development and school learning (UNESCO, 2015). CP has been linked to several lifelong and serious problems, such as physical injuries, anxiety, increased aggression, antisocial behavior, suicide attempts, and drug abuse (Elliman & Lynch, 2000; Gershoff, 2002; Straus & Paschall, 2009; Turner & Muller, 2004). These problems also negatively impact communities as a whole, while local support for CP also enables a cultural of violence, wherein people are encouraged to use physical force to solve problems, rather than using discussion or other more reasonable, fair, or justice-based interpersonal and social strategies. For all of these reasons, corporal punishment is increasingly being banned through legal implements at international and national levels around the world.

In the past, methodological issues were cited to raise questions about the validity of studies showing the many negative impacts of corporal punishment (Baumrind et al., 2002). According to Elliman and Lynch (2000), the link between corporal punishment and child emotional or behavioral problems cannot be proven. This is because it is basically impossible to establish a cause-effect relationship in relation to the effects of CP while holding all other variables constant. On the other hand, that CP is linked to negative effects is also challenged on the grounds that it is hard to identify a direct connection between the absence of CP and positive outcomes to children or to society (Baumrind et al., 2002). Thus, proponents of CP claim that when used appropriately it can have more benefits than harms, for a child and for a community (Larzelere, 2000; Paolucci & Violato, 2004). For instance, Domjan (2000) contends that CP is effective as a means of changing behavior when administered immediately following the occurrence of unwanted behavior, and in a way that clearly and specifically serves to eliminate that behavior. Supporters also may classify CP as mild, moderate, and severe, to defend "mild" and "moderate" forms of corporal punishment. The differences among the categories lie in the amount of force used. To proponents, mild and moderate CP do not cause much if any harm to children (for example, lightly tapping a child's hand or wrist to remind them about their behavior, rather than to cause harm or injury).

Moreover, proponents of corporal punishment argue that parents have moral and cultural rights to nurture their children in the ways they choose. From this view, it is the parent's right to decide what kind of disciplinary actions to take with a particular child in a specific situation. In relation it is further framed by some as an expression of parental love and care for children, rather than as a behavior bordering on or equivalent to abuse (Kim et al., 2000; Yang, 2009). Any effort to take away this so-called parental right is then considered an unnecessary interference in parenting (Dwyer, 2010). Others argue that children are naturally born with evil instincts which make them behave badly. Thus, they claim, CP is an appropriate way for parents to "remove evils" from children (Baumrind, 1996).

However, studies that favor CP, such as that of Baumrind et al. (2002), lack evidence to support their position. Instead, what has been found over time is the ineffectiveness of corporal punishment in childcare and education. In analyzing one case aiming to prove that CP is useful (Thorndike, 1935), Kundu and Tutoo (2012) observed that good behavior was strengthened by the reward that preceded it, while punishment did not necessarily decrease future bad behavior. In addition, the view that CP helps instill discipline does not take into consideration long-term negative consequences. For instance, children can develop feelings of mistrust and become unaffectionate toward punishers over time, while adolescents who are punished are more likely to be in physical and emotional fights with romantic partners later in life (Bachman et al., 2011). CP in educational contexts is consistently linked to school dropout (Mwai et al., 2014). Furthermore, most critics and advocates of corporal punishment share the view that CP should not be the primary method in disciplining children (Ripoll-Nunez & Rohner, 2006; see also Straus & Donnelly, 2005). As we discuss later in this chapter, these and reasons provide significant support for moral and legal arguments against the use of CP at home and in school.

2.2.2 *Theoretical and Empirical Research*

In our research on corporal punishment, ecological theory helps us recognize and position childcare and protection within a family-preschool-society context. From an ecological perspective, corporal punishment and abusive behavior is a result of a complex interaction of personal, sociocultural, and environmental factors (Brower, 1988; Day et al., 1998; Garbarino, 1977; Korbin et al., 1998). An ecological view of CP considers interactions over time within intersecting domains of parents and teachers, and of children and the environment, which includes factors such as family structures and social norms. Elaborating the situation of the child at the microsystem, mesosystem, exosystem, and macrosystem provides a multifaceted theoretical understanding of phenomena such as CP (Sidebotham, 2001).

At the microsystem level there is "a pattern of activities, roles, and interpersonal reactions experienced by the developing person in a given setting with particular physical and material characteristics" (Bronfenbrenner, 1979, p. 22). At a slightly broader level, the mesosystem "comprises the interrelations among two or more settings in which the developing person actively participates (such as, for a child, the relations among home, school, and neighborhood peer group; for an adult, among family, work, and social life)" (Bronfenbrenner, 1979, p. 25). Most families at high risk of child abuse and the use of corporal punishment need intervention at the mesosystem level. Meanwhile, the exosystem includes "one or more settings that do not involve the developing person as an active participant, but in which events occur that affect, or are affected by, what happens in the settings containing the developing person" (Bronfenbrenner, 1979, p. 25). This level includes the existence, availability, and nature of social support and other community-level factors (Jack, 2001; Tolliver, 2004). The macrosystem level involves community norms. In a community where many feel that corporal punishment is acceptable, parents consider it normal. Other factors here include religious beliefs and legal standards.

While most of the early studies on CP were conducted in western countries (Durrant, 1999; Gershoff, 2002; Miller-Perrin & Perrin, 2018; Straus, 2003, 2010), recently there has been an increase in research in other parts of the world, including Asia and Africa (Burton, 2008; Chan, 2008; Lansford et al., 2010; Larzelere, 2000; Man et al., 2017; Wang et al., 2018). Such an increase has been triggered by, among other factors, increasing awareness in the general population about the negative impacts of CP in child development and school learning.

In western countries, there are different views on CP. Whilst some western countries have banned CP, others still support its use. In the United States, corporal punishment is legal in schools in 19 states and in homes in all 50 states (Miller-Perrin & Perrin, 2018; Straus, 1994; Straus & Donnelly, 2005). Rates of CP thus remain high there compared to other western countries. From 2006 to 2007, the United States Department of Education found that 39% of students were subjected to CP at least once by teachers (2008). About 80% of all incidents happened in the states of Alabama, Arkansas, Mississippi, Tennessee, and Texas. The rate of CP is very low in some other states which allow CP in schools, however. For example, in Arizona, Idaho, Indiana, Kansas, and Ohio, the prevalence rate has been reported at less than one percent (USDE, 2008). Recently, the incidence rate of CP has decreased in several states (Florida Department of Education, 2009). Relatedly, the United States Center for Effective Discipline (2010) has estimated that cases of CP across the country decreased by 85% from 1976 to 2006. Increasing awareness of the negative effects of CP, banning CP in schools, and changes in lifestyles have been identified as factors that contribute to these downward trends.

In contrast, Sweden has one of the lowest rates of CP in the world. In a comparative study, Lansford et al. (2010) found that none of the Swedish children participating reported having experienced any "severe" form of CP, such as hitting or beating with a stick or any other implement in the month before the study, while none of the Swedish parents believed that CP was necessary in child rearing. Similar findings were obtained by Bussmann (2009). Unfavorable attitudes toward CP in Sweden date back to 1979, when the Swedish government banned CP in school and at home, making it the first country in the world to do so. In order to effectively implement the law, the Swedish government also provided education on alternatives to CP for families and educators (Bussmann, 2009; Lansford et al., 2010; Modig, 2009).

In Asian countries, the prevalence of CP remains high. This might be associated with favorable attitudes toward the practice from the general population and intersecting cultural beliefs that favor CP in child rearing (Chan, 2008; Chan et al., 2011; Chiang, 2009; Cui et al., 2016; Gao et al., 2017, Kumaraswamy & Othman, 2011; Wang et al., 2018; Yang, 2009). Legal prohibition of corporal punishment is uncommon in this part of the world. Corporal punishment is illegal in Philippines schools, but it is acceptable in homes. Sanapo and Nakamura (2011) found there that 61% of children reported being slapped, punched, or beaten with objects such as belt and sticks by their parents. They also observed that boys were subjected to heavier beatings than girls. This difference was explained in connection to Philippine culture, where boys are expected to be powerful and brave.

In Hong Kong, CP is legal at home, but prohibited in schools, day care centers, and penal institutions. In 2008, Chan found that 21% of children surveyed reported being beaten by parents or guardians in the one month preceding the study. Tang (2006) found that 58% of parents used CP. Again, boys were more often subjected to CP than girls. In Malaysia, 63% of participants reported being beaten, slapped, or whipped by parents. Numerous other studies in Asian countries show that corporal punishment is common and mostly used by parents in child rearing to control children's behavior. Cultural and religious values and laws have been identified as key factors in the continued use of CP in child rearing in this context (Chan et al., 2011; Chiang, 2009; Cui et al., 2016; Jocson et al., 2012; Kitano et al., 2018; Man et al., 2017; Naz et al., 2011; Tiwari, 2019).

Corporal punishment of children in African countries is common and widespread. In many African countries it is legal in schools, homes, childcare centers, and penal institutions (Busienei, 2012; Dawes et al., 2005). Out of 54 sovereign states in Africa, only seven have legally prohibited CP in all settings (Global Initiative, 2012). These countries are Togo (2007), Tunisia (2010), Kenya (2010), Republic of Congo (2010), South Sudan (2011), Cape Verde (2014) and Benin (2015). However, in most African countries, including Tanzania, parents, caregivers, and teachers use CP at schools and homes (Boydell et al., 2017; Dawes et al., 2005; Hecker et al., 2014; Mayeza & Bhana, 2017; Mweru, 2010; Njelesani, et al., 2018; Reyneke, 2018). In one study, the African Child Policy Forum (2010) investigated mistreatment of disabled children in Zambia, Uganda, Senegal, Ethiopia, and Cameroon. They found that across these countries, 27% reported experiencing severe forms of corporal punishment. 54% of that group reported incidences of broken bones and teeth and bruising during corporal punishment. 2% reported being permanently disabled by CP, with 21% reporting related hospitalization.

CP has been constitutionally banned in Kenya (adjacent to Tanzania) since 2001, but it is still used in schools. Teachers cane students for slight mistakes, such as talking to each other during lessons. Sometimes CP is administered in a brutal way that leads to injuries such as cuts, bruises, and even death (Muthiani, 1996). Johnston (2004) revealed that about 60% of students in Kenya experience CP in schools. Another study (Mwai et al., 2014) showed that nearly 80% of teachers used CP in kindergarten classes, and 70% expressed dissatisfaction with the prohibition of CP by the government, and wanted its reintroduction (see also Busienei, 2012).

Findings in South Africa echo those from Kenya. A study by Burton (2008) on the magnitude of CP in primary and secondary schools in South Africa, where CP is illegal in schools and at home, found that approximately 70% and 48% of primary and secondary school students, respectively, experienced CP by teachers or principals. Moreover, about half of primary school children faced CP at home. There it was also revealed that teachers have been reluctant to stop using CP due to parental support. A study of parents in South Africa (Dawes et al., 2005) found that 57% admitted to using CP to discipline their children. The same study also revealed that young children aged 3 to 4 years old were most often subjected to corporal punishment. In this study, parents expressed that they preferred CP, because they believed that children were incapable of "self-discipline," while in a study of secondary school teachers (Maphosa & Shumba, 2010), teachers claimed to be incapable of managing students' discipline without CP.

2.2.3 Factors Influencing the Use of Corporal Punishment

The use of corporal punishment in child rearing and in schools is influenced by multifaceted and overlapping factors. It is particularly influenced by cultural and religious factors (Dawes et al., 2005; Dietz, 2000; Gomba, 2015; Hunter et al., 2000; Khoury-Kassabri, 2010; Korbin, 1980; Kuleana, 1997; Yang, 2009; Youssef et al., 1998). A study by Gomba (2015) in Zimbabwe reported that parents supported the use of corporal punishment in schools on cultural grounds. The parents argued that corporal punishment is in line with their cultural practices. In the United States, Dietz (2000) found that the social acceptability of corporal punishment was also a major reason for it widespread use in some areas, observing that "the roots for the use of force as a discipline technique is found throughout our religious and legal institutions as well as ingrained in the sociocultural foundations of American society."

Furthermore, literature has provided evidence to show that religion, especially Christianity, has an influence on the use corporal punishment in child rearing (Ellison & Sherkat, 1993; Gomba, 2015; Owen, 2005; Socolar et al., 2008). In Zimbabwe, the use of corporal punishment in schools is supported more by Christian parents than other groups (Gomba, 2015). A study by Socolar et al. (2008) found that corporal punishment in child rearing in the United States is primarily supported in the "Bible Belt" by conservative Protestants. According to Owen (2005), conservative Protestants believe that corporal punishment is necessarily to raise obedient children and prepare them for heaven.

Various studies across the globe document other factors increasing the likelihood of people accepting and using corporal punishment. Parents' age is one factor that has been found to influence child rearing practices. According to Dawes et al. (2005), younger parents prefer stricter approaches to childcare than older parents. A study by Kelley et al. (1992) also showed that maternal age correlated with the (decreased) use of CP in child rearing (see also Straus et al., 1995; Straus & Stewart, 1999). Day et al. (1998) also confirmed that the use of corporal punishment decreases as parents grow older (in contrast, see Carswell, 2001).

Studies also reveal that those with lower levels of education are more likely to support CP. Dietz (2000) showed that United States parents with lower levels of education more often used harsher parenting practices such as corporal punishment, arguing that lack of education limited parents' exposure to positive parenting strategies. Sharing similar findings, Youssef et al. (1998) argued that children raised by parents with lower levels of education were at higher risk of engaging in CP. Such findings related to parents' educational level and their use and preference for CP have been echoed around the world in India (Hunter et al., 2000), Kenya (Mwai et al., 2014), Israel (Guttmann et al., 2009), Kuwait (Qasem et al., 1998), Canada (Ateah, 2003), Saud Arabia (Abolfotouh, 1997) Zimbabwe (Gomba, 2015), and South Africa (Dawes et al., 2005).

In terms of the age of children, younger children have been found to be more likely to face corporal punishment than older children in India (Hunter et al., 2000), Scotland (Anderson et al., 2002) Hong Kong (Tang, 2006), Egypt (Youssef et al., 1998) and the United States (Dietz, 2000). In Scotland, Anderson et al. (2002) found that children 3 to 5 years of age were most frequently subjected to corporal punishment by parents. Several factors help explain the decrease in use of corporal punishment with older children. According to Tang (2006), parents perceive that when children grow older, they acquire social skills and cognitive abilities, which enable them to live and behave more in accordance with their parents' expectations. Thus, parents often find that corporal punishment is the most effective way of controlling behavior, particularly of young children. Other methods, such as discussion and reasoning, are sometimes considered inappropriate or useless to use with younger children, compared with older children. However, other studies have found that the severity of corporal punishment in some cases increases with children's age (Straus & Stewart, 1999). Other relevant issues here include children's capacities to fight back or defend themselves from punishment (that is, older children can better defend themselves than younger children), and attitudes about whether younger or older children can better cope with or endure CP.

Studies have also found a connection between parents' gender and use of corporal punishment. That is, mothers use corporal punishment more than fathers (Alampay & Jocson, 2011; Boydell et al., 2017; Dawes et al., 2005; Gershoff, 2002; Mahoney et al., 2000; Sanapo & Nakamura, 2011; Tang, 2006). A study conducted in Israel by Guttmann et al. (2009) found that more mothers (58%) than fathers (22%) reported using corporal punishment to discipline children. However, some studies, especially those conducted in Europe and the United States, have found a slight difference or no difference in the use of corporal punishment between mothers and fathers (Holden et al., 1999; Nobes et al., 1999). These findings could suggest that parents in western countries participate more equally in child rearing, in contrast to societies such as

South Africa, Tanzania, and Uganda, where childcare is often seen as entirely the responsibility of mothers (Dawes et al., 2005; Naker, 2005).

The gender of the child has also been identified as a factor that influences the use of corporal punishment in homes and schools. Studies in diverse countries reveal that boys are at higher risk of being subjected to corporal punishment than girls, and face more severe and physically harmful types of CP (Dawes et al., 2005; Day et al., 1998; Gershoff, 2002; Khuwaja et al, 2018; Mayeza & Bhana, 2017; Straus, 1994; Tang, 2006). However, some studies suggest on the contrary that there is no gender difference in experiences of corporal punishment (Hunter et al., 2000; Straus, 1994). Cultural factors and different gender expectations for boys and girls seem to influence the gendered nature of CP. Youssef et al. (1998) found for instance that boys were more often subjected to CP than girls in schools in Egypt. In relation, in Egypt and many other societies, boys are thought to be "tougher," or to require more "hardening," than girls, while girls are viewed as more delicate and fragile.

Another factor identified in the use of corporal punishment is family size. Researchers contend that parents in larger families (with more children) are more likely to use corporal punishment (Abolfotouh et al., 2009; Dawes et al., 2005; Day et al., 1998; Flynn, 1994; Khoury-Kassabri & Straus, 2011; Xu et al., 2000; Youssef et al, 1998). According to Xu et al. (2000), parents in large families express finding it more difficult to monitor and guide the actions of their children. Studies also find that parents in large families feel more stressed about their parenting responsibilities, alongside other intersecting family, social, and economic responsibilities (Straus, 1994).

Additionally, many studies (Ateah & Durrant, 2005; Chung et al., 2009; Dietz, 2000; Kitano et al, 2018; Qasem et al., 1998; Sanapo & Nakamura, 2011; Straus, 1994, 2010) have found that parents who experienced corporal punishment as children are more likely to use it and support its use. Researchers associate this intergenerational transmission of corporal punishment with social learning theory (Bandura, 1977). This theory advocates that people learn from each other through observation and imitation. Individuals who grow up believing that corporal punishment helped them and molded them into their present shape and status are more likely to support the use of CP with their own children. However, some studies have contrasting results. For example, Clayton (2011) found that parents who feel that they were hurt by corporal punishment develop more negative attitudes toward its use. Those who developed negative views associate it with a lack of parental love and care.

Family socioeconomic status (SES) has also been identified as a factor that influences corporal punishment use. CP is more common in lower-income families (Dawes et al., 2005; Dietz, 2000; Pinderhughes et al., 2000; Straus, 1994; Straus & Stewart, 1999; Tang, 1998; Youssef et al., 1998). Giles-Sims et al. (1995) found that American parents with lower incomes were more likely to use corporal punishment. They also reported that parents who were not employed used corporal punishment more than those who were employed. Parents in lower-income families are more likely to be stressed by economic and family issues. According to Straus (1994), parental stress is also a major predictor of the use of corporal punishment.

2.3   International Legal Frameworks

The United Nations Convention on Rights of the Child (UNCRC) of 1990 and the African Charter on the Rights and Welfare of the Child (ACRWC) of 2003 both focus on promoting children's rights and improving their wellbeing. In relation, the UNCRC states explicitly that "children have the rights to be protected from all kinds of abuse including corporal punishment," thereby equating all forms of CP with abuse. Among other things, the convention and the charter also require the governments of member states to provide for all children, regardless of gender, family status, race, and ability, the right to free and quality primary education. For children to enjoy the right to education, the UNCRC and ACRWC call for member states to specifically abolish the use of corporal punishment in education. Equally, both require member states to abolish corporal punishment in homes and other childcare settings.

These issues are explicitly and clearly addressed in UNCRC Articles 19, 28 and 37, and ACRWC Article 16. UNCRC Article 19(1) provides legal protection for children against abuse, exploitation, and violence, including corporal punishment: "States Parties [are] to establish practical legal, administrative and educational measures for the purpose of protecting children from physical and psychological abuse, negligent treatment and exploitation." Article 28(2) further states: "States Parties shall take all appropriate measures to ensure that school discipline is administered in a manner consistent with the child's human dignity." Moreover, Article 37(a) clearly nullifies the use of corporal punishment in all childcare settings: "No child shall be subjected to torture or other cruel, inhuman or degrading treatment or punishment." Likewise, Article 16(1) of the ACRWC condemns the use of corporal punishment in education and childcare settings: "States Parties shall take specific legislative, administrative, social and educational measures to protect the child from all forms of torture, inhuman or degrading treatment and especially physical or mental injury or abuse, neglect or maltreatment" (UNCHR, 1990).

The UNCRC also requires member states to provide education to the public about the provisions of the convention and its importance in enhancing child safety. Article 42 requires member states "to make the principles and provisions of the convention widely known by appropriate and active means, to adults and children alike." Such public awareness can minimize conflicts in implementation and help children become aware of their rights. This complements the approach to child rights emphasized further in international human rights agreements such as the Universal Declaration of Human Rights (United Nations, 1948), which stipulates that the rights of children should be overtly identified, recognized, and protected, as children are considered "vulnerable human beings," who deserve special protection.

2.4 Moral and Religious Arguments Against Corporal Punishment

As Tillson and Oxley (2020) note, moral rights should constrain and inform legal rights as a more fundamental basis for decision making and protecting of vulnerable persons such as children. In relation, there are essential human rights drawn upon within the UNCRC that ground legal demands to ban corporal punishment across societies. Among these are inherent dignity, which demands that the best interests and self-shaped goals of individuals must come before any other social and community demands (Tillson & Oxley, 2020). In this context, harming children for such reasons as cultivating an obedient society or a manageable classroom environment is unjustifiable, as harm interferes with children's own goals and wishes. Furthermore, the UNCRC draws its case for protecting children based on their having evolving capacities. Children are still developing capacities which they need to protect their own rights in the future. In relation, they have rights to education for self-development and self-direction, and to valuable and harm-free experiences, where their bodily integrity is secure.

Proponents often express that CP is in the best interest of children, helping them develop themselves more fully, and deterring them from behavior which could ultimately harm themselves and others around them. This view aligns with a philosophy that children deserve less rights protection rather than more, in relation to their dependent and developing status. However, such views about CP being in the best interest of children are undermined by facts on the ground. Evidence suggesting that CP "works" in the best interest of children is not convincing, as it is rather the fear and risks of pain and harm associated with CP that may deter children from behavior which they understand may lead to their being punished. Here, children are powerless to learn positive lessons or skills or develop positive attributes from experiencing CP, beyond their working to identify how to avoid the pain, discomfort, distress, and loss of bodily integrity and personal autonomy that accompany (that constitute) CP. An environment of fear is not conducive to education or self-development of capacities. Rather, the fear brought about by CP can thwart positive development growth, through the facilitation of antisocial feelings and dispositions, lack of self-confidence and self-efficacy, interpersonal anxiety and insecurity, a narrow-minded focus on avoiding pain at all costs, and related tendencies and outcomes.

Furthermore, moral philosophers observe that it is unethical to punish students to educate them about rules which they do not understand or have the capacity to voluntarily agree to. As Curren puts it (2000, p. 151; 2020), "the one in a position to educate and punish…is to blame, and not the wrongdoer, if the former did not provide suitable education" for children to exercise capacities for self-governance needed to be able to respond to reasonable rules and expectations. Children who change their behavior due to their being subjected to corporal punishment do not learn to understand through CP that what they did wrong, or how it is wrong. Nor are they in the position to provide consent to experiences of CP (that is, to consent to understanding CP as a useful means to learn things they do not know), as proponents of CP also sometimes contend. (That is, in some cases proponents argue that children themselves may express that they accept or appreciate CP.) Instead, children facing CP are effectively "learning" merely that others' demands related to their behavior come before their own interests and desires. Thus, CP always infringes upon a developing sense of human dignity, self-respect, and personal autonomy.

Some proponents of CP liken it to physical or other forms of deterrence from harm, and related preventative behavior to stop plausible or existing harm to oneself or others: for example, physically pulling a child away from a fight with another child. However, this is a separate matter. Such physical deterrence can be morally justified in the case of immediate, obvious impending harm or risk (for instance, grabbing a child roughly by the arm if they are about to walk into traffic). Yet such deterring or preventative behavior is categorically separate from punishment and should be conceptualized as such; thus, there is no "slippery slope" between such cases for thoughtful, conscientious caregivers and educators. This is indicated particularly in General Comment No. 8 (2006) of the Committee on the Rights of the Child (p. 12):

> 14. The Committee recognizes that parenting and caring for children, especially babies and young children, demand frequent physical actions and interventions to protect them. This is quite distinct from the deliberate and punitive use of force to cause some degree of pain, discomfort or humiliation. As adults, we know for ourselves the difference between a protective physical action and a punitive assault; it is no more difficult to make a distinction in relation to actions involving children. The law in all States, explicitly or implicitly, allows for the use of non-punitive and necessary force to protect people.

> 15. The Committee recognizes that there are exceptional circumstances in which teachers and others, e.g. those working with children in institutions and with children in conflict with the law, may be confronted by dangerous behaviour which justifies the use of reasonable restraint to control it. Here too there is a clear distinction between the use of force motivated by the need to protect a child or others and the use of force to punish. The principle of the minimum necessary use of force for the shortest necessary period of time must always apply. Detailed guidance and training is also required, both to minimize the necessity to use restraint and to ensure that any methods used are safe and proportionate to the situation and do not involve the deliberate infliction of pain as a form of control.

As mentioned previously, corporal punishment is often embraced by traditional cultural and religious communities, and Tanzania is no exception here, as we will see in the next chapters. However, "hitting children and causing them pain is incompatible with the values expressed in most teachings of the world religions [including] respect for human dignity, equality, justice, compassion and non-violence" (Churches' Network for Non-violence [CNNV], 2015, p. 5). Endorsements of CP conflict with common statements of the golden rule across religions, which recognize above all else the inherent human dignity and the right of individuals to be treated in line with their dignity as persons (CNNV, 2015). Relatedly, while religious communities may contend that corporal punishment is acceptable and beneficial to children and society as seen from the perspectives of children themselves, in cultural environments where children are freer to express their own interests (and where CP is not commonly used, encouraged, or taught), children hardly endorse the practice.

In relation, the selective use of religious texts to justify CP can also be challenged from within faith community contexts. The biblical statement most often used to justify CP among Christians is "he who spares the rod hates his son, but he who loves him is diligent to discipline him." However, biblical scholars note that the word for "rod" used in Hebrew here is "shebet," which means a "staff" or "scepter." This tool is used for shepherding (not beating) sheep; if a rod used for beating was intended here, an alternative term ("muwcar") would have been used (CNNV, 2015). Increasingly, religious communities around the world are shifting their practices here, recognizing that there is no compelling religious justification for harming children or causing them any form of pain to educate or care for them. CP is not something encouraged in the model of historical religious figures such as Jesus, and it is increasingly observed to ultimately hurt children and communities, as an unnecessary social practice.

Finally, while some people argue that CP is part of cultural tradition, it is important to recognize that communities' "traditional" and "cultural" practices are not set in stone. In many positive ways, the societies of today look differently from those in the past. While slavery and lack of rights for women were common around the world in the past, and CP with slaves and women used to be legally sanctioned across contexts worldwide, today these practices are universally seen as morally wrong: as deprivations of human rights and dignity and as the cause of needless, serious harms toward vulnerable groups. Tanzanian society has seen and responded to many important political and legal changes over time. As will be discussed in the next chapter, what is now Tanzania used to be a German, and then a British colony, where CP of native Tanzanians by colonialists was firstly sanctioned to demand their unquestioning obedience and inspire their fear toward foreigners on their land. It is in this context that CP was first institutionalized in the society, as a form of legal punishment for Tanzanian adults, while German and British colonialists also encouraged local teachers and parents to use CP liberally with local children. Such practices from the colonial era should be questioned, not treasured, today as Tanzania continues on its path toward greater societal flourishing. The next chapters discuss the historical and contemporary situation of CP in Tanzania in more detail.

2.5   Conclusion

This chapter reviewed research and legal perspectives on corporal punishment, particularly of young children, from a global view. We argued that while there are conflicting views on the use of corporal punishment (CP) generally and with preschool-aged children, the best evidence aligns with the view put forward in the United Nations Convention on Rights of the Child and the African Charter on the Rights and Welfare of the Child, that CP causes needless, serious harms to children and incurs negative repercussions more generally in society. While many continue to view CP as acceptable in line with traditional and religious practices, there are significant moral and religious arguments against CP as well. Against this backdrop, we advocate against the use of CP and aim to understand the use of CP in Tanzania better through our research in order to provide more detailed recommendations to eliminate the practice in the future. The next chapter discusses the historical and current status of CP, especially with young children, in Tanzania.

References

Abolfotouh, M. A. (1997). Behavior disorders among urban school boys in south-western Saudi Arabia. *Eastern Mediterranean Health Journal, 3*, 274–283.

Abolfotouh, M., El-Bourgy, M., Seif El-Din, A., & Mehanna, A. (2009). Corporal punishment: Mother's disciplinary behavior and child's psychological profile in Alexandria, Egypt. *Journal of Forensic Nursing, 5*(1), 5–17.

The African Child Policy Forum (2010). *Childhood scars in Africa: A retrospective study on violence against girls in Burkina Faso, Cameroon, Democratic Republic of the Congo, Nigeria and Senegal.* The African Child Policy Forum.

Alampay, L. P., & Jocson, M. R. M. (2011). Attributions and attitudes of mothers and fathers in the Philippines. *Parenting: Science and Practice, 11*, 163–176.

Anderson, S., Murray, L., & Brownlie, J. (2002). *Disciplining children: Research with parents in Scotland.* Scottish Executive Central Research Unit.

Ateah, C. A. (2003). Disciplinary practices with children: Parental sources of information, educational needs. *Issues in Comprehensive Pediatric Nursing, 26*, 89–101.

Ateah, C., & Durrant, J. (2005). Maternal use of physical punishment in response to child misbehavior: Implications for child abuse prevention. *Child Abuse and Neglect, 29*(2), 169–185.

Bachman, R., Randolph, A., & Brown, B. L. (2011). Predicting perceptions of fear at school and going to and from school for African-American and White students: The effects of school security measures. *Youth & Society, 43*(2), 705–726.

Bandura, A. (1977). *Social learning theory.* Prentice Hall.

Baumrind, D. (1996). The discipline controversy revisited. *Family Relations, 45*, 405–415.

Baumrind, D., Larzelere, R. E., & Cowan, P. A. (2002). Ordinary physical punishment: Is it harmful? Comment on Gershoff (2002). *Psychological Bulletin, 128*(4), 580–589.

Boydell, N., Nalukenge, W., Siu, G., Seeley, J., & Wight, D. (2017). How mothers in poverty explain their use of corporal punishment: A qualitative study in Kampala, Uganda. *The European Journal of Development Research, 29*(5), 999–1016.

Bronfenbrenner, U. (1979). *The ecology of human development: Experiments by nature and design.* Harvard University Press.

Brower, A. (1988). Can the ecological model guide social work practice? *Social Service Review, 62*(3), 411–429.

Burton, P. (2008). *Experiences of school violence in South Africa.* Centre for Justice and Crime Prevention.

Busienei, A. J. (2012). Alternative methods to corporal punishment and their efficacy. *Journal of Emerging Trends in Educational Research and Policy Studies, 3*(2), 155–161.

Bussmann, K. D. (2009). *The effect of banning corporal punishment in Europe: A five-nation comparison.* Martin-Luther-University.

Carswell, S. (2001). *Survey on public attitudes towards the physical discipline of children.* New Zealand Ministry of Justice.

Chan, K. L. (2008). *Study on child-friendly families: Immunity from domestic violence.* University of Hong Kong.

Chan, Y. C., Lam, G. L. T., & Shae, W. C. (2011). Children's views on child abuse and neglect: Findings from an exploratory study with Chinese children in Hong Kong. *Child Abuse & Neglect, 35*, 162–172.

Chiang, C. Y. (2009). Taiwan's ban on corporal punishment: Teachers' perceptions of impact and meanings. *International Journal for Educational Reform, 20*(2), 111–131.

Chung, E., Mathew, L., Rothkopf, A., Elo, I., Coyne, J., & Culhane, J. (2009). Parenting attitudes and infant spanking: The influence of childhood experiences. *American Academy of Pediatrics, 124*(2), 278–286.

The Churches' Network for Non-violence (CNNV). (2015). *Ending corporal punishment of children—A handbook for working with religious communities.* The Global Initiative to End All Corporal Punishment of Children.

Clayton, C. (2011). Contemporary British Chinese parenting: Beyond cultural values. *Childhoods Today, 5*(1), 1–25.

Cui, N., Xue, J., Cynthia, A., Connollya, L., & Liu, J. (2016). Does the gender of parent or child matter in child maltreatment in China? *Child Abuse & Neglect, 54*, 1–9.

Curren, R. (2020). Punishment and motivation in a just school community. *Theory and Research in Education, 18*(1), 117–133.

Curren, R. (2000). *Aristotle on the necessity of public education.* Rowman & Littlefield.

Day, R. D., Peterson, G. W., & McCracken, C. (1998). Predicting spanking of younger and older children by mothers and fathers. *Journal of Marriage and the Family, 60*, 79–94.

Dawes, A., Kropiwnicki, Z., Kafaar, Z., & Richter, L. (2005). *Corporal punishment of children: A South African national survey.* Human Science Research Council.

Dietz, T. L. (2000). Disciplining children: Characteristics associated with the use of corporal punishment. *Child Abuse & Neglect, 24*(12), 1529–1542.

Domjan, M. (2000). *The essentials of conditioning and learning.* Wadsworth.

Durrant, J. E. (1999). Evaluating the success of Sweden's corporal punishment ban. *Child Abuse and Neglect, 23*, 435–448.

Dwyer, J. G. (2010). Parental entitlement and corporal punishment. *Law and Contemporary Problems, 73*(2), 189–210.

Elliman, D., & Lynch, M. (2000). The physical punishment of children. *Archives of Diseases in Childhood, 83*(3), 196–198.

Elliott, A. (2006). Universal early education. *Directions in education, 15*(9), 1–2.

Ellison, C. G., & Sherkat, D. E. (1993). Conservative Protestantism and support for corporal punishment. *American Sociological Review, 58*, 131–144.

Florida Department of Education. (2009). *Trends in discipline and the decline in the use of corporal punishment.* Florida Department of Education.

Flynn, C. P. (1994). Regional differences in attitudes towards corporal punishment. *Journal of Marriage and the Family, 56*, 314–324.

Gao, Y., Atkinson, S., & Xing, L. (2017). Prevalence and risk factors of child maltreatment among migrant families in China. *Child Abuse & Neglect, 65*, 171–181.

Garbarino, J. (1977). The human ecology of child maltreatment: A conceptual model for research. *Journal of Marriage and the Family, 39*(4), 721–735.

Gershoff, E. T. (2002). Corporal punishment by parents and associated child behaviors and experiences: A meta-analytic and theoretical review. *Psychological Bulletin, 128*, 539–579.

Giles-Sims, J., Straus, M. A., & Sugarman, D. (1995). Child, maternal and family characteristics associated with spanking. *Family Relations, 44*(2), 170–176.

Global Initiative to End All Corporal Punishment of Children. (2012). *United Republic of Tanzania—Country report.* Retrieved on September 6, 2015, from http://www.endcorporalpunishment.org/pages/pdfs/states-reports/UR%20Tanzania.pdf.

Gomba, C. (2015). Corporal punishment is a necessary evil: Parents' perceptions on the use of corporal punishment in school. *The International Journal of Research in Teacher Education, 6*(3), 59–71.

Guttmann, J., Lazar, A., & Makhoul, S. (2009). Physical punishment in Christian Arab families in Israel: Attitudes and behavior. *Children and Society, 23*(6), 430–441.

Hecker, T., Hermenau, K., Isele, D., & Elbert, T. (2014). Corporal punishment and children's externalizing problems: A cross sectional study of Tanzanian primary school aged children. *Child Abuse & Neglect, 38*, 884–892.

Heckman, J. J. (2010). Building bridges between structural and programme evaluation approaches to evaluating policies. *Journal of Economic Literature, 48*, 356–398.

Heckman, J. J., & Masterov, D. V. (2004). The productivity argument for investing in young children. *Review of Agricultural Economics, 29*(3), 446–493.

Holden, G. P., Miller, S., & Harris, S. (1999). The instrumental side of corporal punishment: Parents' reported practices and outcome expectancies. *Journal of Marriage and the Family, 61*, 908–919.

Hunter, W., Jain, D., Sadowski, L., & Sanhueza, A. (2000). Risk factors for severe child discipline practices in rural India. *Journal of Pediatric Psychology, 25*(6), 435–447.

Jack, G. (2001). An ecological perspective on child abuse. In *Children in society: Contemporary theory, policy and practice*, eds. P. Foley, J. Roche & S. Tucker. Palgrave.

Jocson, R. M., Alampay, L. P., & Lansford, J. E. (2012). Predicting Filipino mothers' and fathers' reported use of corporal punishment from education, authoritarian attitudes, and endorsement of corporal punishment. *International Journal of Behavioral Development, 36*(2), 137–145.

Johnston, T. (2004). Gender series: The abuse of Nairobi school children, Nairobi: Population communication Africa. *Juvenile Justice Quarterly, 2*, 1–17.

Kelley, M. L., Power, T. G., & Wimbush, D. D. (1992). Determinants of disciplinary practices in low-income black mothers. *Child Development, 63*, 573.

Khoury-Kassabri, M. (2010). Attitudes of Arab and Jewish mothers towards punitive and non-punitive discipline methods. *Child and Family Social Work, 15*, 132–144.

Khoury-Kassabri, M., & Straus, M. (2011). Discipline methods used by mothers: The contribution of ethnicity, socioeconomic status, and child's characteristics. *Child Indicator Research, 4*(1), 45–57.

Khuwaja, H., Karmaliani, R., McFarlane, J., Somani, R., Gulzar, S., & Ali, T. S. (2018). The intersection of school corporal punishment and associated factors: Baseline results from a randomized controlled trial in Pakistan. *PLoS ONE, 13*(10), 20–30.

Kim, D. H., Kim, K. I., & Park, Y. C. (2000). Children's experience of violence in China and Korea: A trans-cultural study. *Child Abuse & Neglect, 24*, 1163–1173.

Kitano, N., Yoshimasu, K., Yamamoto, B. A., & Nakamura, Y. (2018). Associations between childhood experiences of parental corporal punishment and neglectful parenting and undergraduate students' endorsement of corporal punishment as an acceptable parenting strategy. *PLoS ONE, 13*(10), 206–243.

Korbin, J. E. (1980). The cultural context of child abuse and neglect. *Child Abuse & Neglect, 4*(1), 3–13.

Korbin, J. E., Coulton, C. J., Chard, S., Platt-Houston, C., & Su, M. (1998). Impoverishment and child maltreatment in African American and European-American neighborhoods. *Development and Psychopathology, 10*, 215–233.

Kuleana. (1997). *Study on corporal punishment in primary schools in Mara region*. Kuleana Centre for Children's Rights.

Kundu, L. C., & Tutoo, D. N. (2012). *Educational psychology*. Sterling Publishers.

Kumaraswamy, N., & Othman, A. (2011). Corporal punishment study: A case in Malaysia. *Psychology, 2*, 24–28.

Lansford, J. E., Alampay, L., Al-Hassan, S., Bacchini, D., Bombi, A., Bornstein, M. H., & Zelli, A. (2010). Corporal punishment of children in nine countries as a function of child gender and parent gender. *International Journal of Pediatrics, 2010*, 1–12.

Larzelere, R. E. (2000). *Child outcomes of non-abusive and customary physical punishment by parents: An updated literature review* (Unpublished manuscript). University of Nebraska Medical Center, Omaha.

Mahoney, A., Donnelly, W. O., Lewis, T., & Maynard, C. (2000). Mother and father self-reports of corporal punishment and severe physical aggression toward clinic-referred youth. *Journal of Clinical Child Psychology, 29*, 266–281.

Man, X., Richard, P., Barth, B., Lia, Y., & Wang, Z. (2017). Exploring the new child protection system in Mainland China: How does it work? *Children and Youth Services Review, 76*, 196–202.

Maphosa, C., & Shumba, A. (2010). Educators' disciplinary capabilities after the banning of corporal punishment in South African schools. *South African Journal of Education, 30*, 387–399.

Mayeza, E., & Bhana, D. (2017). Addressing gender violence among children in the early years of schooling: Insights from teachers in a South African primary school. *International Studies in Sociology of Education, 26*(4), 408–425.

Meadow, R. (1993). *ABC of child abuse.* BMJ Publishing.

Miller-Perrin, C., & Perrin, R. (2018). Physical punishment of children by US parents: Moving beyond debate to promote children's health and wellbeing. *Psicologia: Reflexão e Crítica, 31*, 16.

Modig, C. (2009). *Never violence: Thirty years on from Sweden's abolition of corporal punishment.* Save the Children, Sweden.

Muthiani, S. M. (1996). *Teachers' attitudes towards corporal punishment* (Master thesis). Moi University, Kenya.

Mwai, B. K., Kimengi, I. N., & Kipsoi, E. J. (2014). Perceptions of teachers on the ban of corporal punishment in pre-primary institutions in Kenya. *World Journal of Education, 4*(6), 90–100.

Mweru, M. (2010). *Why are Kenyan teachers still using corporal punishment eight years after a ban on corporal punishment?* Wiley.

Naker, D. (2005). *Violence against children.* Save the Children, Uganda.

Naz, A., Khan, W., Daraz, U., Hussain, M., & Khan, Q. (2011). The impacts of corporal punishment on students' academic performance/career and personality development up-to secondary level education in Khyber Pakhtunkhwa Pakistan. *International Journal of Business and Social Science, 2*(12), 130–140.

Naudeau, S. (2011). Investing in young children: An early childhood development guide for neighborhood context as predictors of parent involvement in preschool children's education. *Journal of School Psychology, 45*(6), 619–636.

Njelesani, J., Hashemi, G., Cameron, C., Cameron, D., Richard, D., & Parnes, P. (2018). From the day they are born: A qualitative study exploring violence against children with disabilities in West Africa. *BMC Public Health, 18*, 153.

Nobes, G., Smith, M., Upton, P., & Heverin, A. (1999). Physical punishment by mothers and fathers in British homes. *Journal of Interpersonal Violence, 14*(8), 887–902.

Owen, S. S. (2005). The relationship between social capital and corporal punishment in schools: A theoretical inquiry. *Youth and Society, 37*(1), 85–112.

Paolucci, E. O., & Violato, C. A. (2004). Meta-analysis of the published research on the affective, cognitive, and behavioral effects of corporal punishment. *Journal of Psychology, 138*(3), 197–221.

Pinderhughes, E. E., Dodge, K. A., Bates, J., Pettit, G., & Zelli, A. (2000). Discipline responses: Influences of parents' socioeconomic status, ethnicity, beliefs about parenting, stress, and cognitive-emotional processes. *Journal of Family Psychology, 14*(3), 380–400.

Pudaruth, S., & Bahadoor, B. R. (2011). Integrating ICT in pre-primary education: The case of Mauritius. *International Journal of Education, 3*(2), 128–216.

Qasem, F., Mustafa, A., Kazem, N., & Shah, N. (1998). Attitudes of Kuwait parents toward physical punishment of children. *Child Abuse and Neglect, 22*(12), 1189–1202.

Reyneke, M. (2018). Educator accountability in South Africa: Rethink section 10 of the South African Schools Act. *Journal for Juridical Science, 43*(1), 117–144.

Ripoll-Nunez, K. J., & Rohner, R. P. (2006). Corporal punishment in cross-cultural perspective: Directions for a research agenda. *Cross-Cultural Research, 40*(3), 220–249.

Sanapo, M. S., & Nakamura, Y. (2011). Gender and physical punishment: The Filipino children's experience. *Child Abuse Review, 20*, 39–56.

Shonkoff, J. P., & Phillips, D. (2000). *From neurons to neighborhoods: The science of early child development.* National Academy Press.

Sidebotham, P. (2001). An ecological approach to child abuse: A creative use of scientific models in research and practice. *Child Abuse Review, 10*, 97–112.

Socolar, R., Cabinum-Foeller, E., & Sinal, S. (2008). Is religiosity associated with corporal punishment or child abuse? *Southern Medical Journal, 101*(7), 707–710.

Straus, M. A. (1994). *Beating the devil out of them: Corporal punishment in American families.* Lexington.

Straus, M. A. (2003). *The primordial violence: Corporal punishment by parents, cognitive development and crime.* Altamira Press.

Straus, M. A. (2010). Prevalence, societal causes, and trends in corporal punishment by parents in world perspective. *Law and Contemporary Problems, 73*, 1–30.

Straus, M. A., & Donnelly, D. (2005). *Corporal punishment of children in theoretical perspective.* Yale University Press.

Straus, M. A., Hamby, S. L., Finkelhor, D., & Runyan, D. (1995). *Parent-child conflict tactics scales.* University of New Hampshire.

Straus, M. A., & Paschall, M. J. (2009). Corporal punishment by mothers and development of children's cognitive ability: A Longitudinal study of two nationally representative age cohorts. *Journal of Aggression, Maltreatment & Trauma, 18*(5), 459–483.

Straus, M. A., & Stewart, J. H. (1999). Corporal punishment by American parents: National data on prevalence, chronicity, severity and duration in relation to child and family characteristics. *Clinical Child and Family Psychology Review, 2*(2), 55–70.

Tang, C. S. (2006). Corporal punishment and physical maltreatment against children: A community study on Chinese parents in Hong Kong. *Child Abuse & Neglect, 30*, 893–907.

Thorndike, E. L. (1935). *The psychology of wants, interests, and attitudes.* Appleton Century.

Tillson, J., & Oxley, L. (2020). Children's moral rights and UK school exclusions. *Theory and Research in Education, 18*(1), 40–58.

Tiwari, A. (2019). The corporal punishment ban in schools: Teachers' attitudes and classroom practices. *Journal of Educational Studies, 45*(3), 271–284.

Tolliver, R. (2004). *Impact of a childhood history of physical abuse and social support on aggressive behavior, attributions, and affect in male adolescents* (PhD thesis). Northern Illinois University, Dekaib.

Turner, H. A., & Muller, P. A. (2004). Long-term effects of child corporal punishment on depressive symptoms in young adults: Potential moderators and mediators. *Journal of Family Issues, 25*(6), 761–782.

United Nations. (1948). *Universal declaration of human rights.*

United Nations Commission on Human Rights (UNCHR). (1990). *Convention on the rights of the child.* United Nations.

United Nations Committee on the Rights of the Child. (2006). *General comment No. 8: The right of the child to protection from corporal punishment and other cruel or degrading forms of punishment.* United Nations.

UNESCO. (2007). *Strong foundations: Early childhood care and education: EFA global monitoring report 2007.* UNESCO.

UNESCO. (2010). *Reaching the marginalized: EFA global monitoring report 2010.* UNESCO.

UNESCO. (2011). *The hidden crisis: Armed conflict and education: EFA global monitoring report 2011.* UNESCO.

UNESCO. (2015). *School-related gender-based violence is preventing the achievement of quality education for all.* UNESCO.

UNICEF. (2010). *Child disciplinary practices at home: Evidence from a range of low-and middle-income countries.* UNICEF.

United States Center for Effective Discipline. (2010). *Discipline and the law.* Zero Abuse Project.

United States Department of Education. (2008). *Civil rights data collection 2006/2007.* Department of Education.

Wang, F., Wang, M., & Xing, X. (2018). Attitudes mediate the intergenerational transmission of corporal punishment in China. *Child Abuse & Neglect, 76*, 34–43.

World Health Organization. (2005). *Changing cultural and social norms supportive of violent behavior.* World Health Organization.

Xu, X., Tung, Y., & Dunaway, R. G. (2000). Cultural, human, and social capital as determinants of corporal punishment: Toward an integrated theoretical model. *Journal of Interpersonal Violence, 15*, 603–630.

Yang, S. (2009). Cane of Love: Parental attitudes towards corporal punishment in Korea. *British Journal of Social Work, 39*, 1540–1555.

Youssef, R. M., Attia, M. S., & Kamel, M. I. (1998). Children experiencing violence II: Prevalence and determinants of corporal punishment in schools. *Child Abuse & Neglect, 22*(10), 975–985.

Chapter 3
Education and Corporal Punishment in Tanzania

Abstract This chapter describes the research context and historical background for understanding the use of corporal punishment in Tanzanian childcare and education. Policies and laws related to children's rights protection in Tanzania are also discussed here, from the Constitution of Tanzania of 1977, and the National Education Act of 1978, to the Law of the Child Act (2009), which was established to domesticate the United Nations Convention on Rights of the Child and the African Charter on the Rights and Welfare of the Child at the national level. Additionally, the chapter discusses past research on the prevalence of and attitudes toward corporal punishment in Tanzania. Overall, this chapter reveals an ambivalent legal context in Tanzania, where protections for children against abuse and corporal punishment are minimal, while many continue to support corporal punishment, from the grassroots to prominent national leaders.

Keywords History of education · Education policy · Tanzania · Corporal punishment · Punishment · Educational policy · Child's rights · Child abuse

3.1 Historical Context

The education that existed in Africa before the coming of foreigners (travelers, missionaries, traders, and colonizers) is commonly referred to as African indigenous education, or traditional African education. Considered broadly, this education was complex, and differed from one society to another (Kahembe & Jackson, 2020). It varied significantly across the continent, given the tremendous diversity of human history, cultural, and geography. However, common to many such approaches is that the immediate environment determined the nature of the curriculum and the content taught to children, rather than large-scale or institutional planning. The major goals of African indigenous education have generally been to consolidate the community, reinforce cultural solidarity of the community or tribe, understand the world socially and environmentally, preserve cultural heritage, and transmit good behaviors and characteristics, such as unselfishness, obedience, respect, honesty, and endurance (Jackson, 2021; Msimuko, 1987).

Anangisye (2008) has argued that molding character and providing moral values were the main concerns of indigenous education in Tanzania. The education system as a whole before the colonial era focused on good manners, good character, obedience, and respect for authority, elders, peers, and children (Kahembe & Jackson, 2020). There were mainly two methods of teaching: oral lecture and practical methods (Ssekamwa, 1997). At the family level, children were told proper ways of greeting elders, for example, through oral narrations. The practical method was learning by doing: gaining technical skills through being active in social and community practices. However, teaching was also done more indirectly, through folk dances, songs, games, proverbs, riddles, legends, and tales. Information about corporal punishment in precolonial Tanzania is difficult to find. It was likely used to some extent (Mwakikagile, 2000).

Formal schools in colonial Tanganyika (now Tanzania Mainland) were first established by European missionaries in the nineteenth century (Semali & Stambach, 1997). The missionaries came from different countries and religious denominations, such as the London Mission Societies (LMS) and the Church Missionary Societies (CMS) from Britain, the University Mission for Central Africa (UMCA) from Germany, and the White Fathers (WF) and the Holy Ghost Fathers (HGF) from France (Mushi, 2009). The purpose of missionary education was to bring "civilization" and convert natives to Christianity (Mbilinyi, 1973). It was also used as a tool for transmitting western values more broadly. This often entailed a dismissal of local knowledge and values, which was seen to stand in contrast to colonial and western norms and standards. In the words of Marah (2006), missionary education often implied "cultural genocide," as natives were typically forced to abandon their traditional values and beliefs in favor of western culture and Christianity. This education was also teacher-centered rather than student-centered, as the aims of education were drawn from the values of missionaries and colonial authorities, rather than from those of children or local people in the community (Jackson, 2015).

The structure of schooling and the methods and medium of instruction were different from one missionary group to another. However, what was common among all groups was the emphasis on obedience to missionary and colonial leaders and structures. In this regard, corporal punishment (CP) was institutionalized in the colonial era as part of schooling. Children were commonly subjected to CP to force them to comply with school regulations and teacher instructions. The most common type of corporal punishment in missionary schools in colonial Tanganyika was teachers beating students with sticks. Missionary schools also promoted the use of CP to parents, arguing that punishing children was in line with Christian teachings (Masoud, 1986).

The first government school in Tanganyika was established by the German colonial government in 1892 in the Tanga region (Mushi, 2009). The aims of colonial education there were many; however, primary among them was to train a small mid-level workforce to assist in running the activities of the government. Thus, the provision of colonial education in Tanganyika was characterized by high levels of discrimination and segregation among natives, based on geographical location, gender, and social background. Sons from the families of local rulers and other elites were given priority access to education. The reading, writing, and mathematical skills they received in colonial schools after graduation were useful for them to serve the interests of the colonial government but were less relevant within their local environment (Kassan, 2000; Mbilinyi, 1973). The recipients of colonial education were also expected to be loyal and obedient. To attain these objectives, corporal punishment was used (Chigara, 2004). CP in schools, at home, and as punishment in the court of law in Tanganyika during German colonial administration was legally sanctioned by the Imperial Decree of 1895 (Iliffe, 1969, 1979).

The British colonial government in Tanganyika also perpetuated the use of CP in disciplining children in schools and homes and as a legal punishment for adults and juveniles. In 1930, the British colonial government enacted the Corporal Punishment Ordinance. This was the first legal framework enacted to guide the administration of CP across British colonies in Africa. The ordinance explicitly promoted corporal punishment of children in homes and schools to instill discipline and for adults found guilty before a court of law as a sentence for crime (Winterdyk, 2002). This ordinance is still used in Tanzania today, cited as CAP.17 (R.E.2002) of the penal code of Tanzania (Nalla, 2010). The extent and severity of corporal punishment in colonial Tanganyika remain unknown, given an absence of historical empirical studies on this topic. However, anecdotal evidence shows that CP was common and widespread.

Tanzania (then Tanganyika) gained independence from Britain in 1961 under the leadership of Mwalimu Julius Kambarage Nyerere, who became its first president when the country became a republic in 1962. Among the first priorities of independent Tanganyika was education, which was perceived as fundamental for national development. Thus, soon after independence the government passed the Education Act of 1962 (Mushi, 2009). This act repealed and replaced the 1927 Education Ordinance. Among other things, the Act abolished all kinds of segregation and discrimination in the provision of education. In relation, the policy of "Education for Self-Reliance" (ESR) was introduced in 1967. According to Nyerere (1967), the objectives of ESR were to "equip learners with knowledge, skills and attitudes that would make them become responsible members of their respective societies and the country at large."

Since then, the government has taken various measures to improve access to and quality of education (Kahembe & Jackson, 2020). In 1982, President Nyerere appointed the Presidential Commission on Education, commonly known as the "Makweta Commission." This commission was tasked to assess the national system of education and provide suggestions to improve education across the country (Masoud, 1986). The commission is well known for its recommendations on formal provision of preprimary education and the abolition of corporal punishment in schools (Mushi, 2009). Unfortunately, this recommendation was never implemented, however, partly due to wide social acceptance of CP since the colonial era. Meanwhile, formal provision of preprimary education was to take more than thirty more years to establish. Until the twenty-first century, provision of preprimary and early childhood education was confined to the private sector, which operated informally, with no support from the government (Mtahabwa, 2007).

3.2 Legal Framework

3.2.1 The Constitution of Tanzania

The Constitution of Tanzania has a significant role to play in providing legal protection to children from corporal punishment and other inhuman and degrading treatment. Tanzania technically has two constitutions: the 1977 Constitution of the United Republic of Tanzania, which is applicable in Tanzania Mainland and Zanzibar, and the 1984 Constitution of Zanzibar, which is applicable in Zanzibar. The Constitution of Tanzania guarantees every person equal access to education. Article 11.2 states that "every person has the right to access education, and every citizen shall be free to pursue education in a field of his choice up to the highest level according to his merits and ability." This was also replicated in the 1995 Education and Training Policy, which states that the "government shall guarantee pre-primary and primary education as the basic right." Therefore, it could be argued that every person in Tanzania, especially school-aged children, is to be ensured access to quality education.

Furthermore, the Constitution provides protection against cruel, inhuman, and degrading treatment and punishment. The Constitutions of Tanzania and Zanzibar each contain a Bill of Rights, identifying several rights held as basic and fundamental for every person in the country, including children. The Bill of Rights is provided in Chapter One, Part Three, of the Constitution of Tanzania (Articles 12–29). Article 13.6(e) states that "no person shall be subjected to torture or inhuman or degrading punishment or treatment." This implies that children are accorded the same constitutional protection as adult men and women in the country.

Tanzania, being a member of the United Nations and the African Union, ratified the United Nations Convention on Rights of the Child (UNCRC) in 1991 and the African Charter on the Rights and Welfare of the Child (ACRWC) in 2003. According to these agreements, the rights of children should be overtly identified, recognized, and protected in the constitutions of all countries. This is important because children are considered "vulnerable human beings," who deserve special protection. However, the Constitution of Tanzania fails to explicitly provide for or recognize the specific rights of children. In the whole Constitution which contains 152 Articles, none mention the words "child" or "children." In contrast, the rights of children in the neighbouring countries of Kenya and Uganda are explicitly provided in their constitutions. According to the UNCRC, the lack of provision of specific rights makes possible the violation of children's rights. In relation, as we will see here, corporal punishment is still used as a disciplinary strategy in homes and schools in Tanzania, and it is still considered by many to be entirely lawful. In the Bill of Rights, indirect recognition is therefore inadequate for children's legal protection.

In addition, the requirement of the Constitution of Tanzania that international laws should be passed by an Act of Parliament before being incorporated into domestic law for national implementation serves to further delay the protection of children's rights in the country. Tanzania ratified the UNCRC in 1991, but it took eighteen years to establish the Law of the Child Act, to enable its domestic implementation.

This meant that for two decades the UNCRC remained irrelevant in the Tanzanian legal system, even after it was formally ratified. A constitutional amendment could remove this provision, to allow for direct implementation of international human rights treaties in the country, and to avoid delays of justice for children (among others) there in the future.

Meanwhile, the process of incorporating international law into the Tanzanian legal system involves making amendments to the original law. As we will see later in this chapter, changes made to the UNCRC and ACRWC, apparently to adapt them to Tanzania, significantly diminished their primary intent. While both the UNCRC and ACRWC prohibit corporal punishment in schools, homes, and other childcare settings, the Law of the Child Act of 2009, created to enable its domestic implementation, continues to legalize corporal punishment in child rearing and schools.

In 2014, the government of Tanzania under the leadership of President Jakaya Mrisho Kikwete initiated the process of writing a new constitution. For the first time in history, the proposed constitution recognized and clearly specified the rights of the child. Article 50 of the proposed constitution listed rights including quality "education, nutrition, health care, residence, guardianship, and protection from harm and violence." Article 50.1(b) provided legal protection of children from corporal punishment and other inhuman and degrading treatment. However, the process of sanctioning the proposed constitution was suspended by the next regime under the new President John Pombe Magufuli, who repeatedly stated that the new constitution was not and would not be a priority for his government. More generally, President Magufuli had a poor record for respecting and protecting human rights, including the rights of women and sexual minorities, as well as children. For instance, in June 2017 when addressing a rally in Chalinze district, Eastern Tanzania, he commented, "as long as I am president… no pregnant student will be allowed to return to school… After getting pregnant, you are done."

3.2.2 The National Education Corporal Punishment Regulations

According to the National Education Act No. 25 of 1978, corporal punishment is lawful in schools in Tanzania. This Act empowers the ministry responsible for public education to establish regulations that guide administration of corporal punishment in public and private schools in the country. Following the establishment of this Act, in 1979 the Ministry of Education established what is commonly known as the "National Education Corporal Punishment Regulations," to manage the administration of corporal punishment in schools. Up to that time, the British Corporal Punishment Ordinance of 1930 had generally guided the administration of CP in schools in Tanzania, and it is likely that the ordinance serves as inspiration for the new regulations. The aim of introducing the new regulations was to curb what was perceived by educational authorities in the country as the increased number of disciplinary problems among students (Feinstein & Mwahombela, 2010; Global Initiative, 2010).

According to the regulations, corporal punishment is defined as "the act of striking a student on her hand or on his normally clothed buttocks with a light, flexible stick." It also notes: "Corporal punishment should be administered for serious breaches of school discipline or for grave offenses. CP shall be reasonable having regard to the gravity of the offense, age, sex, and health of the pupils and shall not exceed six strokes." In addition, the regulations state that only headmasters, or teachers with the headmaster's written approval, may administer corporal punishment. Finally, the regulations require that "all incidents of corporal punishment must be recorded." In Zanzibar, the Zanzibar Education Act of 1982 further served to formally legalize corporal punishment in schools at the local level. Echoing the nationwide regulations, the law allowed teachers and parents to use "justifiable punishment" for disciplinary and educational purposes. The Government of Zanzibar has since then maintained that corporal punishment is "a legitimate and acceptable form of punishment among the peoples of Zanzibar."

In 2000, the Corporal Punishment Regulations were revised following opposition from human rights activists and other humanitarian groups. The number of allowable strokes was reduced from six to four, and only the school head was authorized to administer punishment (not teachers). Penalties, though not specified, were set for educators who went against these regulations. However, in practice things are quite different. Teachers regularly punish their students, most often going beyond the maximum number of strokes permitted without consultation with the head of school. As will be discussed in depth in the next chapter, this trend is influenced, among other things, by lack of awareness among teachers on regulations governing CP in schools (Hecker et al., 2014; Pounds & Hewison, 2012; Yaghambe & Tshabangu, 2013).

In any case, the government has maintained that corporal punishment should continue to be used for the purpose of maintaining positive behaviour in schools. The regulations even encourage its use to improve the status of schools. For instance, Section 3(1) of the National Education Corporal Punishment Regulations states that "corporal punishment may be administered for serious breaches of school discipline or for grave offenses committed whether inside or outside the school, which are deemed by the school authority to have brought or are capable of bringing the school into disrepute." This confirmation of corporal punishment as a legal practice in the country in 2000 attracted conflicting reactions from educational stakeholders within and outside the country. While supporters have asserted that the continued use of corporal punishment can help maintain discipline in schools and raise student academic performance, local opponents note that corporal punishment has devastating effects on child development and school learning (Feinstein & Mwahombela, 2010; Hassan & Balli, 2013).

3.2.3   The Law of the Child Act, 2009

On November 6, 2009, after extensive debate, the parliament of Tanzania passed the Law of the Child Act (LCA). Later that month it was signed by then President Jakaya Mrisho Kikwete. This was the first law to provide legal protection of children's rights in the country, and it remains the most significant and comprehensive law cataloguing Tanzanian children's rights. The law was formulated in line with four underlying principles of the UNCRC: Rights not to be discriminated against, best interests of the child, survival and developmental rights, and rights to participation. As previously discussed, the LCA has been a steppingstone toward the domestication of the UNCRC and ACRWC.

The LCA has provisions which require protection of children from inhuman treatment, including corporal punishment. Section 13(1) states that, "a person shall not subject a child to torture, or other cruel, inhuman punishment or degrading treatment, including any cultural practice which dehumanizes or is injurious to the physical and mental wellbeing of a child." In Zanzibar, the Zanzibar Children Act of 2011 also states explicitly that "no child shall be subjected to violence, torture, or other cruel, inhuman or degrading punishment or treatment or any cultural or traditional practice which dehumanizes or is injurious to his physical and mental wellbeing."

However, the LCA and the Zanzibar Children Act (ZCA) also contain ambiguous interpretations of corporal punishment. For example, Article 13(2) of the LCA empowers parents to use "justifiable punishment" for the purpose of disciplining their children. Similarly, the ZCA gives legal power to parents and guardians to use "reasonable" corporal punishment for the purpose of disciplining their children, stating that "parents may discipline their children in a justifiable manner which shall not amount to injury to the child's physical and mental wellbeing." What is considered a "justifiable manner" is not defined by the Acts. Due to cultural and individual differences, what is held as reasonable by one parent may not necessarily be seen as reasonable by another. What might be regarded by some as justifiable in one situation might not be justifiable in another situation. Therefore, the use of such subjective terms in legal pronouncements can lead to confusion and inconsistency, resulting in generally weak standards for protecting children. Furthermore, according to Tanzanian law, parents have legal exemption from being prosecuted in the case that corporal punishment leads to "minor" physical injury to children. This is all contrary to the UNCRC, ACRWC, and the Bill of Rights in the Constitution of Tanzania.

The government is also not clearly committed to implementing or monitoring the LCA (or the ZCA). There is no apparent strategy for assessing implementation of the LCA (or the ZCA). The United Nations established the United Nations Committee on the Rights of the Child to monitor implementation of the UNCRC, while the African Union established the African Committee of Experts on the Rights and Welfare of the Child to monitor implementation of the ACRWC. In Tanzania, a committee of a similar nature, responsible for monitoring national implementation of the LCA (and the ZCA), has not been established or developed. Instead, responsibility has been placed vaguely under the different organisations of the Ministry of Health and Social Welfare, the Ministry of Community Development, Gender and Children, and the

Ministry of Constitution and Legal Affairs. There is no formal coordination, or roles or responsibilities specified for implementation or assessment of the LCA, for any of these ministries.

Among the other challenges in the implementation of the LCA (and the ZCA) is the use of English language in legal documents. For many years, English has been used as the official language in Tanzania's legal system. Almost all laws in Tanzania are written in English, without being translated into Swahili language, which is the language of the majority, or other local languages. This situation has contributed significantly to a lower level of understanding of laws among key stakeholders in society. For example, most parents who participated in our study were unable to read, write, or communicate in English effectively. English is not commonly used by ordinary people in Tanzania. In this context, it is difficult for Tanzanian people to understand the LCA or its implications in an independent manner.

During the parliamentary debate on the LCA, many members of the parliament raised their voices against any attempt to abolish the use of corporal punishment in child rearing or education. Many argued specifically that the LCA was an external (western) intrusion upon traditional practices. For example, Paul Peter Kimiti, a member of parliament for the Sumbawanga constituency said, "the law should do it as a matter of necessity to guard our culture and traditions against western interference. We are not obliged to follow western culture" (Hansard, 2009). Similarly, Zabein Muhaji Mhita, a member for Kondoa North constituency, was quoted saying, "corporal punishment is the most effective parenting strategy; it has been used across generations in our homes and schools to promote discipline… corporal punishment was sanctioned by both Quranic and Christian teachings as an appropriate disciplinary strategy" (Hansard, 2009).

The Minister of Community Development, Gender and Children thus stated:

> On the basis of the research which was conducted by the Law Reform Commission of Tanzania, the majority of the citizens preferred a reasonable chastisement as a method of correcting and disciplining children. Hence we order that a child should neither be corporally punished in a degrading manner, nor should corporal punishment exceed limits. Section 13 of the bill puts limits while administering corporal punishment. One should take into account age, health and understanding of a child. (Hansard, 2009)

The government therefore largely authorized the continued use of corporal punishment with the introduction of the LCA. As the next chapter shows, the belief that the abolition of corporal punishment is based on western philosophies of child rearing was also expressed by many participants in our study.

3.3 Prevalence of and Attitudes Toward Corporal Punishment in Tanzania

It is unsurprising that in this context corporal punishment has been and remains prevalent in homes and schools in Tanzania (Frankenberg et al., 2010; Hassan & Balli, 2013; Hecker et al., 2018; Kaltenbach et al., 2018; Komba, 2015; Kuleana, 1999;

UNICEF, 2011). One study revealed that 95% of primary school children in Tanzania had experienced CP in schools (Hecker et al., 2014). About 82% experienced "severe" forms of CP, such as being beaten with sticks, belts, or other implements, and nearly 15% had at least once been seriously injured by CP, to the extent that they required medical treatment. UNICEF (2011) relatedly found that about 75% of children in Tanzania are subject to corporal punishment at school. The incidence type and rate of CP differs from one child to another. Some children reported being kicked, whipped, or slapped more than six times by their teacher in one month.

A more recent situational analysis conducted by the Tanzania Institute of Education in collaboration with UNESCO (2021) in Ilala (Dar-es-salaam) and Sengerema (Mwanza) gathered data from 4,655 students about school-related violence including CP. They found that 43% of students reported that they were beaten "most of time" by their teachers in the past month, while another 30% reported they were beaten by their teachers "all the time" (Tanzania Institute of Education [TIE], 2021). Furthermore, 37% of students reported observing their fellow students being beaten by their teachers regularly (TIE, 2021).

According to past research, parents, teachers, and students have somewhat divided views on the use of CP in child rearing in Tanzania. However, many parents and teachers have expressed strong support for its continued use (Feinstein & Mwahombela, 2010). Kuleana (1997) found that teachers in primary schools preferred corporal punishment, because they felt it was easy to administer. This study also found that Tanzanian teachers had less training on alternative forms of discipline. Today, teacher education curriculum discusses restricting the use of CP and all other forms of violent punishment, and it also has topics on child rights and child abuse. Nonetheless, more than 85% of parents and 65% of students still express support for corporal punishment in child rearing and education (Kuleana, 1997; Yaghambe & Tshabangu, 2013).

A recent study conducted by the Tanzania Institute of Education (TIE, 2021) and UNESCO found that when CP was used without giving children explanations about why they were being punished, CP was not in any way effective for behavior management. As an intervention, the TIE worked with teachers to better understand why they used CP and encouraged them to use alternative methods of discipline. In this case, teachers claimed that they used CP because they themselves had experienced CP as students; therefore, they saw CP as the best practice for correcting children's behavior. Learning alternative techniques in this context, to not depend upon CP, was seen as effective in the study for reducing the use of CP in Tanzanian schools (TIE, 2021).

However, despite the potential for using alternative, more effective forms of school-based discipline, in different periods of Tanzania's history, top government officials, including the President, have continued to explicitly support the use of corporal punishment in schools. In 2013, when launching an educational program in Dar es Salaam, the Deputy Minister for Education and Vocational Training Philipo Mulugo said that corporal punishment would continue to be instituted in public schools, noting that "the move to re-introduce caning in schools would attract a lot of criticism, especially from those who call themselves human rights activists"

(AllAfrica, 2013). Some former ministers of education have also made similar statements. When addressing the public in Dodoma at the end of "Education for All Week" then Minister of Education Margareth Sitta stated, "caning of stubborn students in primary and secondary schools is mandatory and it is supported by the law" (Haki Elimu, 2011).

In January 2015, when the Tanzania Ministry of Education appeared before the United Nations Committee on the Rights of the Child (the body responsible for monitoring implementation of the UNCRC), it denied the existence of corporal punishment in Tanzanian education. In its statement, it at the same time indicated that caning is allowed in schools in Tanzania, in accordance with the "traditional culture" of child rearing. This perspective is contrary to the definition of corporal punishment provided by the Committee. The Committee defines corporal punishment as "any punishment in which physical force is used and intended to cause some degree of pain or discomfort, however light." Meanwhile, the United Nations has made it clear that no kind of corporal punishment, however "mild," should be tolerated. Therefore, the Committee ordered the government to "explicitly and entirely prohibit any kind of corporal punishment of children by law, even in cases of so-called reasonable chastisement within the family."

Nonetheless, when addressing a rally in his hometown of Chato in north-western Tanzania in 2017, then President Mgufuli stated, "I am wondering why they stopped caning in schools. I was also caned and that's why I am standing here today" (Human Rights Watch, 2017). As mentioned previously, in 2019, he publicly "congratulated" a regional commissioner shown in a viral media video caning a group of schoolboys one by one, adding that "I told him that he didn't beat them hard enough" (Ng'wanakilala, 2019). Such comments can prompt the continued, if not increased, use of corporal punishment in schools. In this context, some teachers in our study indicated that they did not believe there were any useful or valid corporal punishment regulations, at the international or national level, given the president's own strongly voiced views.

However, there has been no major research examining the views of parents and teachers regarding the use of corporal punishment with young and preschool-aged children, despite the significance of early childhood development and preschool education for a person's success in later life, and for the development and positive wellbeing of communities more generally. In the next chapter, we present the findings of our study related to the prevalence of and attitudes toward corporal punishment with young children, among parents, teachers, and educational policy makers in Tanzania.

3.4 Conclusion

Although it is unclear how and to what extent CP was used to discipline children in precolonial Tanzania, during the colonial period CP was encouraged and institutionalized through law. After independence, CP has effectively remained legal. Parents and teachers are allowed to punish their children by force as a way of apparently disciplining them, without facing any repercussions for potential harms inflicted in the process.

Both the UNCRC and ACRWC focus on promoting children's rights and improving their wellbeing across member states. By sanctioning the UNCRC and ACRWC, Tanzania placed itself in a position to fulfil and implement the provisions of the Convention and the Charter. However, as discussed, due to the dualistic nature of the Tanzanian legal system, international laws cannot be enforced directly in the Tanzanian court of law. Instead, international legal instruments must be transformed and incorporated into domestic laws to gain legal status for national implementation. To domesticate the UNCRC and ACRWC, Tanzania passed the LCA. The LCA (and the ZCA) stand as the legal framework and guideline for safety of children in Tanzania against all kinds of mistreatment. Yet they do not stand against corporal punishment. Parents are still privileged by the law to use CP under the umbrella of instilling discipline to their children, which is contrary to the international agreements of which Tanzania is a signatory.

In sum, corporal punishment is still regarded as legal in homes and across educational and childcare settings. It is also still used as a punishment in the court of law for young offenders (Global Initiative to End All Corporal Punishment of Children, 2010). No law in the country has effectively required parents or guardians to refrain from using CP. And even recently established laws have failed to prohibit the use of CP, at homes, schools, or childcare institutions. The next chapter explores the reality of CP in Tanzania in more detail, with an analysis of the findings from our own research with parents, teachers, and policy makers.

References

AllAfrica. (2013, April 9). *Tanzania Daily News* (Dar es Salaam). AllAfrica.

Anangisye, W. (2008). Moral education and character development: Learning from the African indigenous education framework. *Journal of Adult Education Tanzania, 16*, 1–23.

Chigara, B. (2004). *Land reform policy: The challenge of human rights law*. Ashgate Publishing.

Feinstein, S., & Mwahombela, L. (2010). Corporal punishment in Tanzania's schools. *International Review of Education, 56*, 399–410.

Frankenberg, S. J., Holmqvist, R., & Rubenson, B. (2010). The care of corporal punishment: Conceptions of early childhood discipline strategies among parents and grandparents in a poor and urban area in Tanzania. *Childhood, 17*(4), 455–469.

Global Initiative to End All Corporal Punishment of Children. (2010). *Corporal punishment of children in the United Republic of Tanzania*. Retrieved on March 14, 2015, from http://www.end corporalpunishment.org/pages/frame.html.

Haki Elimu. (2011). *Litigating the right to education in Tanzania: Legal, political, and social considerations and potential applications*. Haki Elimu.

Hansard. (2009). Parliament of Tanzania. Speech by Paul Peter Kimiti in Parliamentary Debates on the Law of the Child Bill in Dodoma. 4 November 2009.

Hassan, A. H., & Balli, T. A. L. (2013). Assessing the effects of corporal punishment on primary school pupils' academic performance and discipline in Unguja, Zanzibar. *International Journal of Education and Research, 1*(12), 1–12.

Hecker, T., Hermenau, K., Isele, D., & Elbert, T. (2014). Corporal punishment and children's externalizing problems: A cross sectional study of Tanzanian primary school aged children. *Child Abuse & Neglect, 38*, 884–892.

Hecker, T., Goessmann, K., Nkuba, M., & Hermenau, K. (2018). Teachers' stress intensifies violent disciplining in Tanzanian secondary schools. *Child Abuse & Neglect, 76*, 173–183.

Human Rights Watch. (2017). *"I had a dream to finish school": Barriers to secondary education in Tanzania.* Human Rights Watch.

Iliffe, J. (1969). *Tanganyika under German rule 1905–1912.* Cambridge University Press.

Iliffe, J. (1979). *A modern history of Tanganyika.* Cambridge University Press.

Jackson, L. (2015). Challenges to the global concept of student-centered learning with special reference to the United Arab Emirates: 'Never fail a Nahayan.' *Educational Philosophy and Theory, 47*(8), 760–773.

Jackson, L. (2021). Purposes of education. In W. Thompson (Ed.), *Philosophical foundations of education.* Bloomsbury.

Kahembe, J., & Jackson, L. (2020). *Educational assessment in Tanzania: A sociocultural perspective.* Springer.

Kaltenbach, E., Hermenau, K., Nkuba, M., Goessmann, K., & Hecker, T. (2018). Improving interaction competencies with children—A pilot feasibility study to reduce corporal punishment. *Journal of Aggression, Maltreatment and Trauma, 27*(1), 35–53.

Kassan, Y. (2000). Julius Kambarage Nyerere. *Prospects: The Quarterly Review of Comparative Education, 24* (12), 247–259.

Komba, S. C. (2015). How research and theories of learning inform government on the issues related to the use of corporal punishment in schools. *Journal of Philosophy, Culture and Religion, 6*, 7–12.

Kuleana. (1997). *Study on corporal punishment in primary schools in Mara region.* Kuleana Centre for Children's Rights.

Kuleana. (1999). *The state of education in Tanzania.* Kuleana Centre for Children's Rights.

Marah, J. K. (2006). The virtues and challenges in traditional African education. *The Journal of Pan African Studies, 1*(4), 15–24.

Masoud, A. (1986). *History of formal education in Tanzania.* University of Dar es Salaam Press.

Mbilinyi, M. (1973). Education in Tanzania with gender perspective. *Papers of Education and Development (PED), 2*, 17–35.

Msimuko, A. K. (1987). Traditional education in pre-colonial Zambia. *Journal of Adult Education and Development, 29*, 21–32.

Mtahabwa, L. (2007). *Pre-primary educational policy and practice in Tanzania: Observations from urban and rural pre-primary schools* (PhD Thesis). University of Hong Kong.

Mwakikagile, G. (2000). *Africa and the West.* Nova Science Publishers.

Mushi, A. K. P. (2009). *History and development of education in Tanzania.* Dar es Salaam University Press.

Nalla, M. K. (Ed.). (2010). *Crime and punishment around the world, Volume I: Africa and the Middle East.* ABC-CLIO.

Ng'wanakilala, F. (2019, October 5). Tanzanian president backs official who beat students with a stick. *Reuters.*

Nyerere, J. K. (1967). *Education for self-reliance.* Government Press.

Pounds, R., & Hewison, M. (2012). *Addressing violence against children in schools in the United Republic of Tanzania.* Commonwealth Education Partnership.

Semali, L., & Stambach, A. (1997). Cultural identity in an African context: Indigenous education and curriculum in East Africa. *Folklore Forum, 28*(1), 1–25.

Ssekamwa, J. C. (1997). *History and development of education in Uganda.* Fountain Publishers.

The Tanzania Institute of Education & UNESCO. (2021). *Connect with respect: Curriculum for improving learning environment through building skills for respectful and non-violent relationship in Tanzanian schools.* Tanzania Institute of Education.

The United Republic of Tanzania (1977). *The constitution of the United Republic of Tanzania.* Government Printer.

The United Republic of Tanzania (1978). *The National Education Act, 1978,* Act No. 25 of 1978. Government Printer.

The United Republic of Tanzania. (2009). *The law of the Child Act.* Government Printer.

UNICEF (2011). *Violence against children in Tanzania: Findings from a national survey 2009.* UNICEF.

Winterdyk, J. (Ed.). (2002). *Juvenile justice system: International perspectives.* Canadian Scholars' Press.

Yaghambe, R. S., & Tshabangu, I. (2013). Disciplinary networks in secondary schools: Policy dimensions and children rights in Tanzania. *Journal of Studies in Education, 3*(4), 42–56.

Chapter 4
Findings on the Use of Corporal Punishment

Abstract This chapter presents the major findings of our study, about the use of and attitudes towards corporal punishment in homes and preschool settings in the Dodoma Urban District, Tanzania, based primarily on interview and questionnaire data with parents and educators. It also presents findings about factors that influence the use of corporal punishment based on our data. Our study shows that corporal punishment is commonly used with young children in our research sites. We additionally elaborate five subthemes related to its use: cultural norms and religious beliefs, psychosocial and demographic factors, teachers' qualifications and parents' level of education, past experiences with corporal punishment, and beliefs about the effectiveness of corporal punishment. Finally, the chapter provides findings about attitudes toward, and knowledge of the national and international legal framework related to corporal punishment among parents, teachers, and educational policy makers.

Keywords Tanzania · Corporal punishment · Young children · Early childhood education · Preschool education · Teacher perceptions · Parent attitudes · Educational policy · Children's rights

4.1 The Use of Corporal Punishment with Young Children

4.1.1 Parents

In our study, parents were asked to indicate the type(s) of disciplinary strategies they used to discipline their young children at homes. The responses to questionnaires showed that 81% of parents reported using (physical) corporal punishment as their primary method of discipline and behavioral management and control. We also found that the use of corporal punishment was slightly higher among parents of children in public schools (87%) than among those whose children attended religious schools (78%) or international schools (78%).

Verbal punishment was also extensively used among parents according to their reports, although to a lesser extent than corporal punishment (CP). During interviews, many parents stated that verbal punishment was not harmful to the child. As one parent commented, "children cannot be hurt by the words of mouth. In fact, most parents shout at their children in an attempt to warn them against their behaviors. The only strategy that brings desirable results is physical punishment." Scolding was reported by 62% of parent participants. This was followed by name calling (54%), grounding (38%), ridicule (35%), and threatening (27%). In addition, other strategies, such as withdrawal of privileges and ignoring, were reported by 46% and 42% of parents, respectively.

On the other hand, it was found that in addition to the use of corporal punishment some parents also employed positive parenting strategies. In particular, the use of rewarding was common among parents of children in religious preschools (78%), international schools (67%), and public schools (63%). This was followed by directing (46%), discussion (34%), and guidance and counseling (27%). Overall, similar strategies for punishment were used by parents of children across school types. The summary of these findings is provided in Table 4.1.

Parents were also asked to indicate the types of corporal punishment they used. The responses showed that hitting their children with objects such as sticks and belts was most common, with approximately 58% of parents on average reporting it as their most used method. This was followed by slapping (54%), pinching (42%), twisting or pulling ears (38%), smacking (31%), punching or shaking (8%), and denying food (4%). Here, we found significant discrepancies in strategies used among parents of children in public versus religious and international preschools, which normally reflects the socioeconomic status of the family (see Table 4.2).

We were also interested to know how frequently parents used corporal punishment. The findings (see Table 4.3) show that about 19% of parents used it "always"; 38%

Table 4.1 Disciplinary strategies used by parents

Disciplinary strategies	Public preschools (%)	Religious preschools (%)	International preschools (%)	Average (%)
Corporal punishment	87	78	78	81
Scolding	63	56	67	62
Name calling	63	44	56	54
Withdrawal of privileges	25	44	67	46
Ignoring	50	33	44	42
Grounding	50	44	22	38
Ridicule	50	22	33	35
Threatening	38	22	22	27
Rewarding positive behaviors	63	78	67	69
Directing	38	44	56	46
Discussion	25	33	44	34
Guidance and counseling	25	22	33	27

Table 4.2 Corporal punishment strategies used by parents

Disciplinary strategies	Public preschools (%)	Religious preschools (%)	International preschools (%)	Average (%)
Hitting by using objects	75	44	56	58
Slapping	63	56	44	54
Pinching	50	33	44	42
Twisting/pulling ears	50	44	22	38
Smacking	38	22	33	31
Punching/shaking	13	11	0	8
Denying food	13	0	0	4

Table 4.3 The frequency of use of corporal punishment by parents

Disciplinary strategies	Public preschools (%)	Religious preschools (%)	International preschools (%)	Average (%)
Always	25	22	11	19
Sometimes	38	44	33	38
Rarely	25	11	33	23
Never	13	22	22	19

indicated using it "sometimes"; 23% said they used it "rarely"; and another 19% reported to have never used corporal punishment. Again, differences can be seen based on the school type.

4.1.2 Teachers

Teachers also indicated the types of punishment they used in questionnaires. The responses indicated that most teachers (80%) reportedly used corporal punishment to discipline their students. This was followed by non-physical punishment such as verbal punishment (57%), time out (52%), detention (38%), threatening (24%), and reporting to the head of school (19%) Meanwhile, about 20% of teachers from all school types reported that they also used positive disciplinary strategies. The most common methods were directing (71%), rewarding positive behaviors (67%), discussion (48%), and guidance and counseling (43%). As seen in Table 4.4, some variation across school types can be seen here.

Among forms of corporal punishment, caning was reported as most common. On average, 76% of teachers reported using canes to hit preschoolers. This was followed by slapping (52%), pinching (52%), smacking (33%), and twisting or pulling ears (33%). The questionnaire also revealed the use of some other types of corporal

Table 4.4 Disciplinary strategies used by teachers

Disciplinary strategies	Public preschools (%)	Religious preschools (%)	International preschools (%)	Average (%)
Corporal punishment	87	83	71	80
Verbal punishment	63	67	43	57
Time out	38	50	71	52
Detention	38	33	43	38
Threatening	25	17	29	24
Reporting to the school head	13	33	14	19
Directing	75	83	57	71
Rewarding positive behaviors	50	67	86	67
Discussion	38	67	43	48
Guidance and counseling	25	50	57	43

punishment: requiring students to stay in an uncomfortable position (47%), engage in manual labor (43%), engage in excessive physical exercise (10%), and stand outside in the sun for a long period of time (5%).

Again, some differences are seen in strategies used among teachers based on school type. The summary of these findings is provided in Table 4.5.

Table 4.5 Corporal punishment strategies used by teachers

Disciplinary strategies	Public preschools (%)	Religious preschools (%)	International preschools (%)	Average (%)
Caning	88	67	71	76
Slapping	63	67	29	52
Pinching	50	50	57	52
Stay in an uncomfortable position	75	33	29	47
Manual labor	63	50	14	43
Twisting or pulling ears	25	33	43	33
Smacking	38	33	29	33
Excessive physical exercise	13	17	0	10
Standing in the sun	13	0	0	5

Table 4.6 The frequency of use of corporal punishment by teachers

Disciplinary strategies	Public preschools (%)	Religious preschools (%)	International preschools (%)	Average (%)
Always	25	17	29	24
Sometimes	38	33	29	33
Rarely	25	33	14	24
Never	13	17	29	19

Regarding frequency, 33% of teachers reported using corporal punishment "sometimes" to discipline students. About 24% said they used it "rarely," and another 24% indicated "always" using corporal punishment to discipline students. 19% said they "never" used corporal punishment. Notably, frequencies for teachers and parents of children in public preschools are the same here, while differences again can be seen based on school type. Table 4.6 provides a summary.

Overall, minor differences can be seen in the use of corporal punishment of children in public versus private preschools (including religious and international preschools). The use of corporal punishment is more prevalent in public schools. Similarly, at homes, corporal punishment is reportedly more common in families whose children attend public preschools than in those attending private preschools. The next section discusses the more in-depth views and attitudes of parents and teachers and other interrelated factors influencing their use of corporal punishment with young children.

4.2 Attitudes Toward Corporal Punishment and Other Major Factors

4.2.1 Cultural Norms and Religious Beliefs

83% of parents and teachers who responded to questionnaires, and the majority of teachers and parents who were interviewed described corporal punishment in child rearing as a cultural norm. They explained that corporal punishment had been used in society across generations, and that they viewed it as part of their cultural heritage. One parent puts it thusly: "Our forefathers used corporal punishment to maintain discipline among children; the method yielded positive results as there was more peace and harmony in the society, and children respected elders and adhered to other cultural and traditional values." Most parents and teachers interviewed emphasized that in Tanzania, it was culturally acceptable for parents and other elders to punish children when they misbehaved. Parents claimed to have cultural "rights" and authority to administer corporal punishment to misbehaving children. Both parents and teachers also believed that it was an acceptable and effective way of teaching discipline. As one father said, "our culture not only supports the use of corporal punishment in child rearing, but it also encourages it."

During interviews, some parents talked about how the use of corporal punishment helped them maintain discipline in their families and thereby contributed to upholding the cultural values of the society. Parents believed that it was also necessary for raising disciplined children who would themselves be good parents in the future. As one mother put it, "how else can children learn good behaviors, respect our cultural values, and respect their parents and other elders in the society without serious corporal punishment?" Another mother noted:

> Some parents these days are actively contributing to the erosion and deterioration of our traditional values and norms. They do not punish their children when they misbehave; they are treating them like eggs. In the long run this will risk the whole society. But as far as I know, such kinds of parents are very few in the community where I live.

In relation, parents expressed that it was their duty to instill cultural values to their children from an early age. In this context, it is regarded as a matter of shame to the family if children are disrespectful to elders, reflecting that parents failed to instill important cultural values to their children. As one mother said:

> I feel ashamed and in fact, it is shameful to the entire family, when my child shows bad behavior in front of other people. I must punish him right away, because if I don't do so, my reputation as a parent in the society will be jeopardized. People will say that I do not know how to raise disciplined children. This will have negative impacts in the future to the whole family.

Traditionally, a good family name is important for the future prosperity of a family, because it is associated with other social attributes such as marriageability. In other words, people prefer to plan for their children to marry others coming from a reputable family, who are seen to publicly honor cultural and traditional values. On the other hand, parents stated that children would not respect adults in the public sphere in the absence of corporal punishment.

Interviews with teachers revealed that corporal punishment was also common in preschools, particularly public preschools where teachers regarded it as an important element of school culture. Teachers reported that corporal punishment was required to maintain discipline and create a conducive environment for teaching and learning. Additionally, during interviews some teachers expressed that corporal punishment in school was in conformity with the African culture of child rearing. They argued that the school is part of the society, and that therefore what happens in schools reflects what happens in the society. As one teacher explained:

> As a school, we have the duty to train and nurture our students in line with the existing cultural norms and values. Since corporal punishment is part of our cultural values, then, it is our responsibility as teachers to promote its use for the betterment of our children and the whole society at large.

Most teachers also noted that corporal punishment was widely used in homes to control "children's bad behaviors." Teachers reported that most parents supported its use in schools. They also said that children who do not respect their parents were more likely to disrespect their teachers. Thus, they argued, collaborative efforts were needed to manage children. As one teacher remarked, "in this school we work together with parents to discipline our students; sometimes parents bring their children and ask teachers to put discipline in their heads." Most parents interviewed also supported the use of corporal punishment in schools on cultural grounds, reflecting on their own school days. Many argued that when they were in school CP was common and widely used. Therefore, they said, they grew up believing that corporal punishment was an integral part of school culture. Some even expressed shock that someone would bother to discuss or study corporal punishment in schools, as they saw it as entirely normal. As one mother said:

> Corporal punishment was used throughout my school years, particularly at primary and secondary school levels. As a matter of fact, it helped me a lot with my education; I believe it can also help my children and even my grandchildren to fulfill their educational dreams.

Others said that corporal punishment was an important cultural asset necessarily to create peace and tranquility in society. Both parents and teachers argued that the current apparent "moral breakdown" in Tanzania is the result of some parents and teachers refraining from corporal punishment. One teacher recalled an incident that happened during the period of our study. Some schoolboys from a secondary school invaded a neighboring village and harmed villagers. The teacher said that this incident and others of the same nature occurred because parents and teachers were not effectively using corporal punishment to discipline and control children: "The increase of social problems in the community as we see today can be associated with failure of parents to use corporal punishment effectively. Parents these days are busy trying to become their children's best friends instead of being real parents."

4.2.2 Psychosocial and Demographic Factors

The analysis of our data indicates that participant attitudes toward and use of corporal punishment intersect with psychosocial and demographic factors. These factors include family/class size, family socioeconomic status, the child's gender and age, and the parent's gender and age.

4.2.2.1 Family/Class Size

Responses from parents in our study revealed that parents with many children preferred corporal punishment more strongly than parents with fewer children. Parents commonly associated having many children with increased tension, anger, stress, and frustration. This apparently compelled them to use corporal punishment, to obtain immediate compliance and as a means of providing stress relief. As one mother put it, "I have four children; they cause me headaches all the time, especially during the weekend, when they don't go to school. When I get angry, I punish them."

In interviews, parents explained that it was difficult for parents with many children to use positive parenting strategies. They argued that in practice positive parenting strategies required more time and resources to be successful. As one mother commented:

> I have five children; they have different needs and different interests. Therefore, it is very difficult to monitor them individually, to meet the needs and interests of every child. Besides, I have other responsibilities as well, so I cannot spend the whole day just looking after my children. What will they eat? When they misbehave, I use sticks to put discipline in their head.

Thus, other methods were considered too time consuming. As another mother put it:

> I was raised in a family of eight children. My parents, especially my father, used to punish us severely. I think he was stressed by family responsibilities. On my side, I have only two children; I can manage their behavior very well without using corporal punishment. When you have many children, four or more I think, corporal punishment can be better.

The preference for and use of corporal punishment also increased with the rise in the number of students in a class. Nearly 33% of teachers interviewed said that they used CP in their preschool classes. They cited an overcrowded class as the main reason. Similarly, more than half (52%) of teachers stated in questionnaires that the use of corporal punishment was necessary especially for teaching in a large class. In public preschools, the number of students per class is said to normally range from 60 to 80, while in private preschools it ranges from 25 to 40. Through observations, we also found that the number of students in a classroom in public preschools was 60 to 80, while in private preschools the class sizes ranged from 20 to 35. The educational policy makers we interviewed also expressed concerns regarding class size and the use of corporal punishment. As one remarked, "we are currently having a very serious problem of shortage of teachers in our schools. Teacher-students ratio has been increasing yearly; this situation has increased problems in managing children's behaviors." A teacher from a public school aired a similar opinion, claiming, "if I were teaching in a small class of 20–30 students, I would probably not use corporal punishment during the teaching and learning process, because it is easy to manage and control students in such a small class."

4.2.2.2 Family Socioeconomic Status

We found a robust association between family socioeconomic status (SES) and parents' use of corporal punishment. Responses from questionnaires indicated that about 75% of parents whose monthly income was below 500,000 Tanzanian shillings (approximately 225 USD) used corporal punishment frequently to discipline their children. On the other hand, 24% of parents with a monthly income above 1,000,000 Tanzanian shillings (approximately 500 USD) used corporal punishment. Increasing family responsibilities coupled with economic hardship were also cited as stressors for low-income parents, that compelled them to use corporal punishment. One mother commented:

I have 4 children, but unfortunately my husband is a very busy person. Therefore, I am the one responsible for taking care of the kids, preparing them for school, cooking, shopping, and doing all other family chores. These activities make me feel angry and stressed most of the time. Hence, I am always using corporal punishment as a means of controlling my children.

In our study, parenting stress was expressed as higher among parents from low-income families than among others. Parenting, economic, and social stresses were associated by parents with financial difficulties, excessive home chores, and other family responsibilities. This in turn reportedly had an impact on the relationships between parents and children, and the way parents were able to respond to child discipline issues. As one parent explained, "I have so many things to do; I have to work in order to contribute to family income. Therefore, when my children misbehave, I usually use corporal punishment to put discipline in their heads."

On the other hand, parents from high-income families were found to have less stress about parenting issues. Most of them also showed greater tolerance for their children's perceived misbehaviors. Moreover, parents with higher levels of income were found to be more knowledgeable about positive parenting strategies. These parents argued that corporal punishment was not the only effective way of combating children's problematic behavior. They called for alternative methods such as motivation, discussion, and counseling. This situation could be linked to the greater ability of higher income families to access various sources of parenting information, such as books, magazines, and childcare specialists. Meanwhile, we found that parents in low-income families had little access to parenting information, especially on alternative and positive discipline. During an interview, a mother from a high-income family was quoted as noting, "as parents, we can correct our children's behaviors through reasoning, talking, counselling, and positive reinforcement. Corporal punishment should be used as a last resort."

Some parents from low-income families also expressed that they punished their children because they were unable to provide for their basic needs. During the interviews, some parents said that they sometimes got upset and responded harshly when their children asked them to buy things they could not afford, such as toys, bikes, new clothes, and food and drinks like soda, biscuits, yoghurt, and chocolate. These items were considered expensive, luxurious, and unnecessary. Spending money on such items was interpreted by most parents from low-income families as a misuse of family income. This, in turn, had an impact on parent–child relationships. In this regard, one mother from a low-income family commented, "when I don't have money and my child asks me to buy her a toy or new clothes for her birthday, I get distressed, and I beat her." Moreover, parents reported that these situations often resulted in quarrels. These quarrels were perceived by many parents from low-income families as signs of child disobedience. As a result, they reacted by adopting punitive measures.

Responses to questionnaires and interviews also showed that unemployed parents used corporal punishment more frequently than employed parents. Many unemployed parents spent most of their time at home with their children. This increased the possibility of conflicts with their children. A mother had the following comment here:

"When I was working with [anonymized] company, I hardly punished my children, but since my contract was terminated, my punishing behavior has increased."

The use of corporal punishment was also higher in public preschools than in private preschools. Most children in public preschools come from low-income families. Our analysis of teachers' interview responses showed that at times children were punished for reasons related to poverty, and not because of their disobedience or "bad behaviors," as some claimed. For example, in observations, we saw that children were punished for not wearing proper school uniforms and for not having exercise books or pencils. This was arguably the result of the families' inability to provide school materials for their children. Thus, living in a poor family increased the likelihood of being subjected to corporal punishment at preschool. During an interview, one mother noted, "my six-year old son stopped going to school, because teachers used to beat him because he wore an improper school uniform." While students in public preschools were punished for not wearing proper uniforms or for not having writing materials, their fellows at religious and international preschools were freely provided these materials (due to parents paying school fees).

4.2.2.3   Child Gender

Parents who responded to questionnaires and who were interviewed reported that boys were subjected to more corporal punishment than girls. And it was indicated that boys were subjected to more severe types of corporal punishment, such as being beaten with objects like a stick or a belt. Parents reported that girls were subjected to "lighter" kinds of corporal punishment, such as pinching and smacking. Parents associated these differences with expected gender roles in society. Boys were expected to be the head of the family, and leaders of the community, whereas girls were to prepare to become future wives and mothers, who would not operate beyond the family.

In relation, one mother said, "I punish boys very hard using sticks and sometimes belts; this is because the future of the family lies in their hands. But for girls, one simple slap is enough. Girls should be protected from getting scars, or else their bride price will be low." A mother of a child from an international preschool likewise stated that it was not culturally encouraged to hit girls severely, because that was likely to affect her femininity and reduce her possibilities for getting married: "No man would marry a woman with scars on the whole of her body. Therefore, as parents, we should always be very careful when we want to use corporal punishment to discipline our daughters." These answers also suggest that severe, scarring, injurious forms of corporal punishment would be the norm for girls, as it is for boys, without these gendered expectations in mind.

Boys were reportedly subjected to more corporal punishment because they were believed to engage in more disruptive behaviors. As one mother remarked, "boys are more active and disrespectful than girls; therefore, if you don't hit them more seriously at a younger age, they will become uncontrollable in the future, when they grow older." Another similarly stated, "girls are easier to control than boys.

Most of the time they stay and play at home, and they can also respond quickly to parents' instructions." We also found that boys were reportedly punished more often by their fathers, while girls were punished more often by their mothers. A father who was interviewed stated that he always tried to avoid using corporal punishment to discipline his daughters. In his own words, "girls are physically weaker than boys; they are also very delicate by nature, and therefore, they should be handled and treated with care." A mother similarly expressed that "because of their biological composition, girls should not be punished severely like boys."

However, we also found that these differences in using corporal punishment with girls and boys were not as common in the age bracket of 0 to 6 years old. Many expressed in this context that the care of young children was primarily the responsibility of the mother. In this connection, one father remarked, "I usually don't punish young children below the age of 8. These should always be under the care of the mother. Just imagine a man like me rising my hand to punish a child of age 3. No, that will never happen."

4.2.2.4   Child Age

Our analysis revealed that children in the age group of 0 to 6 years old were at higher risk of corporal punishment than older children. Almost 71% of parents who responded to questionnaires indicated that their young children (2 to 6 years old) were more often subjected to corporal punishment than their children in other age groups. Parents also expressed that the use of corporal punishment increased in terms of frequency and intensity for children from 3 to 10 years old. Children aged 3 to 10 years old were considered particularly troublesome, hyperactive, and naughty. As one mother said:

> This is the time when children start schooling and get opportunities to mingle with other children. Unfortunately, they may learn bad behaviors and impolite language from their fellow children. As a parent, you need to take deliberate measures to prevent this from happening to your child before it is too late. The use of corporal punishment is one such measure.

Moreover, during interviews, most parents argued for the use of corporal punishment from the earliest stage possible, to "put discipline in children's heads." They supported their arguments by citing a Swahili proverbs, *mkunje samaki angali mbichi*, meaning "bend the fish while it is still fresh." As one mother stated, "young children should be disciplined until when they become old enough to be able to differentiate good from bad."

However, some mothers explained that infants and toddlers should be subjected "only" to "lighter" forms of CP, such as pinching, slapping, and smacking. Older children (5 years old and above) were to be subjected to "stronger" forms of corporal punishment, such as caning, whipping, and paddling. According to these parents, young children were punished for the purpose of threatening, warning them not to repeat the same mistake again. As one mother remarked, "if you don't slap these young children seriously, they will keep on repeating the same mistakes over and over again." Another parent voiced a similar view: "I used to hit my two year old son because he was crying unnecessarily; when I gave him a light slap on his mouth, he would keep quiet immediately." Behaviors such as playing, lack of concentration, and restlessness, which are common to almost all young children, were interpreted as "bad behaviors" by parents in our study. Therefore, to stop such behaviors, parents saw corporal punishment as essential.

These views were also supported by preschool teachers. They believed that preschool children in particular should face corporal punishment because they are incapable of understanding and interpreting instructions. Teachers cited the age of children and their level of cognitive understanding as major factors. During interviews, teachers from all types of schools agreed that older children faced less corporal punishment than preschool children. They said that the use of alternative methods was not suitable with preschool children, because such methods involved higher mental functions, such as thinking and reasoning. As one teacher explained:

> The use of alternative methods such as talking, discussion, guidance, and counseling require high abilities of reasoning and analyzing things critically. This is not possible with preschool aged children. I think this is the reason why teachers preferred the use of corporal punishment with preschool aged children.

Moreover, preschool teachers, like parents, asserted that it was difficult to manage preschool children without corporal punishment. Teachers explained that preschool children were overactive in the sense that it was difficult to control their behaviors. Likewise, they asserted that it was difficult for young children to concentrate on one task without being punished or threatened. One teacher from a private preschool remarked:

> Preschool children are very stressful; without CP you will not manage them. You can tell them it is time for readings, but they will want to go out to play. So as a teacher, if you are not careful, children will not be able to read. Parents and the school management will blame you for the failure, and at a private school like this you can even lose your job.

4.2.2.5 Parent Gender

Both mothers and fathers who participated in our study believed that corporal punishment was necessary in child rearing. Our study revealed that both used corporal punishment. However, we found some differences in fathers and mothers' perceptions and practices. As previously mentioned, there was generally greater acceptability of corporal punishment by mothers than by fathers. More than 66% of parents who were interviewed and almost 84% of those who responded to questionnaires expressed that mothers used corporal punishment more than fathers. This difference could be linked to the norm that in Tanzania, mothers are held more responsible for child rearing.

During interviews, both mothers and fathers explained that according to African tradition mothers were the primary care providers for children. Thus, they had a duty to nurture, discipline, and shape the behaviors of their children in line with family and societal norms, values, and standards. Interestingly, all mothers who were interviewed maintained that it was more the mother's duty than the father's to be involved in parenting young children. They argued that the father would be more involved when the child got older. In this regard, one mother commented:

> A father is an authority figure in the family. Therefore, culturally, it is not advisable for a father to deal with young children's issues, particularly with ones involving discipline, because by doing so he will be undermining his authority. A father normally gets involved when a child enters the adolescent stage.

4.2.2.6 Parent Age

We found that parents who were aged 35 years old or younger used and favored the use of CP more than counterparts who were older than 35 years old. Responses from questionnaires showed that more than 67% of parents under 35 years old were in favor of the use of corporal punishment. They said that in comparison with other methods such as discussion and positive reinforcement, corporal punishment was more effective. It is also possible that younger parents preferred the use of corporal punishment due to a lack of parenting experience. As one elderly mother stated, "parenting is the hardest activity that any parent will ever have; it has never been easy particularly for young parents." Another mother (46 years old) shared her own experience with using corporal punishment over time:

> When I was in my late twenties and early thirties, I used to punish my children quite often; I would punish them every time they misbehave. But today, when I reflect back on those years, I can certainly conclude that my punishing behavior was motivated by a lack of parenting experience. As a parent, you need to talk to your children, listen to them, and explain things to them in a polite and loving manner. However, I am uncertain if young parents have the necessary capability and skills of doing this activity very effectively and efficiently without using corporal punishment.

During interviews, older parents argued that parenting was a very challenging activity that required a high level of patience and tolerance. In addition, they were found to be more considerate and have more positive attitudes towards children. During one interview, an older parent stated, "my experience showed that parents become mentally flexible with age, they become more tolerant towards their children's behaviors."

Compared to older parents, younger parents were more likely to use corporal punishment based on their holding high expectations for their children's behaviors and success in life. During interviews, young parents explained that they expected their young children to have a high level of self-control, self-discipline, and obedience; to be respectful to elders; to perform well in school; to perform various physical tasks effectively; and to be able to judge correctly right from wrong in different contexts. They said that they wanted their children to live a meaningful, better life than they had. However, they felt that this would not be easy unless they used strict parenting approaches. In this regard, one parent remarked:

> I must acknowledge myself that I am a very strict parent; I punish my children regularly when they misbehave. However, this does not mean that I do not love them, but it is because I want the best for them.

Similarly, a 25 year old mother of two commented:

> I want my children to perform well in school, because this is the only viable way which can guarantee them success in their future life. So, I am always very sensitive to their school performance; when they score low grades, I punish them.

4.2.2.7 Parents' Level of Education

Parents with lower levels of education (primary and secondary education) more strongly supported the use of corporal punishment compared to counterparts with university degrees. These parents had the view that the best and most effective way of teaching discipline was through corporal punishment. In supporting their views, they asserted that the pain that a child experienced due to corporal punishment served as a reminder to them not to misbehave again. One parent said, "some parents treat their children like eggs, this is not good. Children should be treated harder so that in the future they will not bring shame to the family." Also, less educated parents argued that corporal punishment was necessary so that children behave well and have respect for parents, teachers, and other adults in the community. In this regard one mother, a primary school graduate, asked, "how can our children learn good behavior, obedience, and respect for adults without serious punishment?".

On the other hand, these kinds of arguments were criticized by parents with university or postgraduate degrees. They argued that to raise well-mannered and disciplined children, parents should stop using punitive methods. Instead, they suggested parents should adopt participatory, non-punitive parenting strategies, such as coaching and discussion. One father, a university graduate, said, "I don't punish my son, I talk to him instead." His views were supported by another parent with an undergraduate education, who argued that rewarding and taking away privileges was the best way of shaping the behaviors of preschoolers. Likewise, more well-educated mothers reported using less corporal punishment to enforce discipline. They said that they used positive parenting strategies such as discussion, coaching, and positive reinforcement. When we asked where they learned about positive parenting, most replied that they learned about positive parenting indirectly while in postsecondary institutions. Others said they learned about positive parenting informally through social media and interactions with friends and colleagues. One mother said:

> I learned about child development at the university when I was studying for my bachelor's degree. But also in our community, we have several NGOs, such as UMATI, which help to educate parents and the general community about different aspects related to child development, parenting, and sexual and reproductive health education.

Another mother shared similarly, "I am a member of a WhatsApp group where we discuss different child-related issues and other family affairs. This group has been very useful to me; it has helped me to understand how to raise my children well."

4.2.2.8   Teachers' Qualifications

In parallel, we found that teachers with a "Grade A" teaching certificate, the minimum qualification required to practice teaching in pre-primary and primary schools in Tanzania, had more favorable attitudes towards corporal punishment than their colleagues with higher qualifications, such as diplomas and university degrees. In the public preschool, where most teachers held Grade A certificates, the use of corporal punishment was more common than in the private preschools, where teachers had higher qualifications. Most teachers in our study who held a Grade A certificate justified their use of CP on the ground that it was administered with good intentions, for the purpose of shaping the behaviors of students. Also, according to these teachers, the overall aim of using corporal punishment was to create a conducive classroom environment for teaching and learning. Moreover, they reported that the use of corporal punishment was accepted and encouraged by parents. One teacher from a public preschool commented, "it is common in this community; parents ask teacher to discipline their children so that they can concentrate on their studies."

Most teachers (67%) with a Grade A certificate disliked the use of alternative methods of discipline. They argued that alternative methods were less effective, particularly for teaching preschool children. Also, 33% of teachers from this group said they were unfamiliar or uncomfortable with the use of alternative methods in disciplining children. During an interview, one teacher from a public preschool stated:

> I cannot waste my time and energy talking to preschoolers when they misbehave; they won't understand. So, I usually let the stick talk on my behalf. Corporal punishment teaches children a lifelong lesson that can never be achieved by using soft words.

In addition, some of these teachers argued that young children were not intellectually ready to conceptualize and understand the meaning of other disciplinary methods such as counseling, advice, or rewarding. As one said, "if you are a teacher and you do not punish your students, they will never respect you. In my school it is hard to find a single teacher who does not punish students." Likewise, such teachers reported they were compelled to use corporal punishment because of time constraints. During interviews, they stated that they had many things to cover within a limited period. In this situation, they argued, it was difficult to use alternative methods to deal with unruly students during class: "When students are making noise in class during the teaching and learning process, the simplest and easiest way to deal with them is through the use of CP." Another teacher voiced the same view:

> Teaching in preschool classes is very hectic; young children are very stubborn. Corporal punishment has helped me to maintain discipline in my class in such a way that I have been able to continue with my normal teaching activities smoothly and cover the syllabus on time.

Teachers with higher teaching qualifications, such as diplomas and university degrees, had different views. Most suggested that corporal punishment should be used as a last resort. They also advocated for the use of alternative methods for disciplining students. These teachers expressed that CP was associated with psychological and physical consequences which negatively impacted learning. As one teacher from an international preschool said:

Corporal punishment is not an appropriate disciplinary strategy. When it is used in classrooms during the teaching and learning process, it always distracts students' attention, leading to failure instead of success. Also, some students' bodies have become so accustomed to it that it is no longer effective.

4.2.2.9 Parents and Teachers' Past Experiences of Corporal Punishment

More than 75% of parents who participated in this study reported that they were subjected to corporal punishment by their parents during childhood. During interviews, many parents (63%) who were subjected to corporal punishment during childhood expressed that they approved of the strategy. One mother said, "my parents caned me every time I made a mistake; I am also punishing my children in the same ways that my parents did to me." However, there were a few parents who evaluated their childhood experiences with corporal punishment more negatively. Though they were subjected to corporal punishment during childhood, they did not have positive attitudes toward it. For instance, one father of two explained that corporal punishment was commonly used in his family, which caused him to dislike the method. He said:

> My father was a very cruel person. He used to beat me and my sibling very harshly, especially when he was drunk. I remember one day my mother intervened in order to help us, but she was beaten too. This experience gave me a negative look on corporal punishment. I hate it.

Many women in Tanzania are victims of physical and sexual abuse and violence. Unfortunately, many cases are not reported to law enforcement agencies, because they are perpetrated by husbands, and hence considered family matters.

Additionally, many teachers (72%) stated that their past school experiences with corporal punishment influenced them to use CP to discipline students. All teachers who participated in this study expressed that they were subjected to corporal punishment when they were students. During interviews, some teachers and educational policy makers argued that they saw the corporal punishment they received in school as useful to shape their character and get them to where they are today. As one teacher from an international school shared, "although it happened a long time ago, I can still remember very clearly how corporal punishment transformed my ways of conduct, from being a naughty boy to a well behaved and responsible student." Many teachers also associated their academic achievements with the corporal punishment they received in school.

Teachers explained that they were punished because they did not follow teachers' instructions or school regulations. Therefore, they said that the punishment they received was their fault. As one teacher from a public school said, "I cannot blame a teacher who punished me in school; he was in the process of fulfilling his duties." She thus argued that students who misbehaved should be punished, so that they could feel the consequences of their misbehaviors. She emphasized that corporal punishment was the best option for teaching good behavior to students. Further, teachers stated that they grew up believing that corporal punishment was an acceptable way of teaching good behavior. One teacher from an international school remarked, "during my childhood corporal punishment was normal; if you are a child and you misbehave, you should expect to be punished by anyone." On the same note, teachers expressed that strict class control was pivotal for effective learning.

4.2.3 Views About the Effectiveness of Corporal Punishment

Parents and teachers who had positive attitudes about corporal punishment expressed above all else that it was an effective disciplinary strategy. Many parents, mainly of children in public schools, expressed that children who were not exposed to corporal punishment were troublesome, causing discomfort in their homes. Furthermore, they believed that the absence of corporal punishment was detrimental to the child's future. They thus argued that corporal punishment was needed to raise obedient and disciplined children. Moreover, they insisted that the use of corporal punishment was effective in the sense that it helped children to live a meaningful life, by abandoning bad behaviors. During an interview, a mother commented, "corporal punishment is the only disciplinary strategy that is feared by almost all children; this makes it more effective."

In addition, parents felt that corporal punishment was an ideal child rearing strategy for a globalized world. They mentioned in this context that children today are exposed to television and the internet. Thus, they said, strict parental control accompanied by corporal punishment was necessary to raise disciplined children in what they saw as an increasingly challenging world. As one mother put it, "techno-logical invention, especially the internet, is spoiling our children; it exposes them to adult content. As a parent, if you are not careful in controlling your children, they will have sex, take alcohol, and smoke before they are ready."

In relation, many parents cited examples from western countries, where they said that children were rude and undisciplined, because parents in those countries were reluctant to use corporal punishment. A father remarked here: "Children in western countries do not respect their parents; they use impolite language when talking to their parents, and sometimes they report their parents to the police when parents used punitive strategies to discipline them." A mother also added in her defense of CP, "look at the western societies today: the level of moral erosion and social unrest is increasing at an alarming rate." Thus, they associated what they saw as moral decay in western countries with the failure of parents to use corporal punishment. Parents from high-income families also shared these attitudes.

These were also supported by most teachers in our study. Teachers stated that corporal punishment was effective in managing and controlling students' behav-iors in the classroom and at preschool more generally. Many believed that without corporal punishment, it would be difficult to control students during class. Most teachers across types of preschool argued that students who were subjected to CP behaved better and had better academic records compared to counterparts who were not subjected to CP. And they reported that students behaved appropriately because of fear of CP. A teacher remarked: "Corporal punishment is very effective; it makes students change their bad behaviors. I am calling upon the government to rethink its decision to regulate the use of corporal punishment in school." Additionally, most teachers maintained that corporal punishment helped them perform their teaching duties smoothly and effectively.

Although some teachers reported that corporal punishment should be or is used only for (apparently) serious offenses, such as fighting or the use of impolite language, we observed that most teachers commonly used it in dealing with minor offenses as well, such as students talking during the teaching and learning process. In preschools, many teachers used teacher-centered strategies. In this context, it is considered deviant for students to speak during class without a teacher's permission. Any student who violates this rule is immediately subjected to punishment—usually CP. As one teacher commented, "I don't entertain children who talk during class hours without my permission. A good students should sit and listen carefully to teacher's instructions."

All heads of school who were interviewed also supported the idea that corporal punishment was effective. Like parents and other teachers, they said that it was difficult for schools to handle student behavioral problems without CP. As the head of a religious private school commented, "from my personal beliefs and understanding, corporal punishment is still the most effective way that can be used to maintain discipline in our schools." However, all heads of school interviewed indicated they were aware of the regulations that governed the administration of corporal punishment. Yet, they maintained that corporal punishment was the only disciplinary strategy that could effectively control students' behaviors. The head of a public school explained:

> I usually turn a blind eye when my teachers use corporal punishment to discipline students without following the required procedures as stipulated in the corporal punishment regulations. I know what they are doing is for the benefit of the students, school, and society at large. Teachers do not use corporal punishment unnecessarily.

Moreover, during interviews, heads complained about the difficulties of maintaining order in preschool in the absence of corporal punishment. They argued that without corporal punishment, it would be difficult to manage the school, especially one which included students from diverse sociocultural and economic backgrounds. As the head of a religious school put it, "I think in a multicultural school, corporal punishment is the best and the most effective disciplinary strategy that can help to manage and control the behavior of the students towards a common goal." In this case, we found that alternative methods of discipline were rarely used in schools or in homes. While teachers stated that such methods were not effective in schools, parents said they had no faith in "soft" approaches. As one parent remarked, "these modern approaches are less effective; experiences showed that they have not eradicated disruptive behavior in homes and schools even in the western world."

Some also argued that the use of corporal punishment was effective particularly when disciplining students with special educational needs (SEN). Teachers believed that due to their unique behavioral and learning characteristics, it was difficult to use alternative methods to manage and control the behavior of students with special educational needs, such as those with attention deficit hyperactivity disorder. Therefore, they reported that CP was more effective than other methods in reducing unacceptable behaviors among such students. Most teachers (76%) agreed that CP was effective in promoting desirable behaviors among students with SEN. Some heads also agreed. The head of a public school commented, "corporal punishment improves students' behaviors, especially for those students who are prone to behavioral problems, such as those with emotional and behavioral problems or attention deficit hyperactivity disorder."

However, a few teachers (19%) saw CP as ineffective. They argued that corporal punishment did not influence students' behavior in all situations. Some said that corporal punishment did not instill discipline, but instead led to feelings of anger and fear. Moreover, it was argued that corporal punishment facilitated no intrinsic motivation, which was important in maintaining long-lasting positive behavior change. As one educational policy maker said, "corporal punishment becomes effective when it is administered reasonably. But unfortunately, some teachers and even parents use it in an inappropriate way; hence it does not contribute to behavior change." Likewise, a few parents said that corporal punishment was not an effective strategy, particularly in inculcating a sense of self-discipline. In this regard, one parent noted:

> Children do not learn how to behave by being punished; punishment has a kind of extrinsic motivation, which is not recommended in teaching children self-discipline. In order for children to internalize self-discipline and develop the skills and abilities for self-control, they need an intrinsic kind of motivation which can be obtained through teaching and not punishment.

The same parent argued that to raise self-disciplined children, it was important for parents to treat their children with respect and dignity. She insisted on building a strong and positive parent–child relationship, which she saw as vital in keeping children on the right path.

4.3 Attitudes Regarding Corporal Punishment Law and Policy

4.3.1 Parents

Most parents (63%) who participated in our study were not aware of the existence of the Law of the Child Act (LCA), the law meant to protect children in Tanzania from abuse in line with the United Nations Convention on Rights of the Child (UNCRC) and the African Charter on the Rights and Welfare of the Child (ACRWC). Most (58%) who indicated being aware of the LCA held negative perceptions about it. They stated that the LCA conflicts with cultural norms and practices of child rearing. In this case, they continued to cherish what they regarded as their traditional norms of corporal punishment. For example, during an interview, a father commented:

> I think the establishment of this law did not take into account the cultural values and norms of our society. This law provides over-protection of children's rights. This is not acceptable, and it is against our traditional practices of child rearing. Children should always be under the control of their parents.

Many parents also suggested that the government ratified the UNCRC and established the LCA to please the international community, and to fulfil international donor requirements to secure funding, such as those of the United Nations Children's Fund (UNICEF). During interviews, parents expressed that the government should not be driven by external pressure to sign international agreements. Instead, they felt that such international influences went against the best interest of Tanzanian people, including Tanzanian children. Further, they asserted that external influences were associated with conditions that were not healthy for the country's sovereignty. Throughout interviews, parents thus referred to anti-corporal punishment policy as an outside agenda with no good intentions or potential for the country. As one parent remarked:

> As a country we must be careful with laws which originate from outside our country, as some of these laws may not be relevant to us, and others may have the goals of disrupting our civilization. We should always understand who we are and be proud of what we are. We should not be influenced by external values, but we should preserve and carry forward our own traditions and culture.

Some parents whose children attended private preschools suggested that it was important for the government to strengthen its partnership with parents, particularly at the grassroots levels, to bring about desired social transformation. They said the LCA would not function effectively in this context, where many parents and the community at large still had positive attitudes toward corporal punishment. During an interview, a mother commented:

> The government should educate parents, and partner with them in order to improve the lives of children. Laws against child abuse and corporal punishment in particular will not function effectively unless parents and the general public are made aware of the intent of laws.

In relation, another parent remarked, "the policymaking process does not involve key stakeholders, such as parents and teachers. This may explain why the law is strongly opposed by parents and teachers."

Parents also had the view that the LCA was likely to increase unnecessary misunderstandings between parents and children. During interviews, most parents who were aware of the LCA expressed concerns about it leading to moral decay. They expressed that unlike the "good old days," children now were disrespectful, rude, and uncontrollable. They blamed the government for enacting laws like the LCA, which provided "over-protection" of children. One older mother expressed here that the government should not tamper with "family matters": "A strong family lays a good foundation upon which we build the future of the country." Dramatically, in her eyes implementing laws such as the LCA could lead to the collapse of the society.

Responses from parents also reflected that there were no formal educational means for them to learn about the LCA and other child protection policies, such as the

UNCRC and ACRWC. Most relied on informal means to obtain information about child protection policies. Parents' responses also indicated limited understanding about other child protection policies, such as the Child Development Policy of 1996, the Sexual Offense Special Provision Act of 1998, and the Education and Training Policy of 2014. This suggests that little has been done to educate the community about child protection law. Low levels of understanding of child protection policies and legal guidelines among parents can also indicate a lack of political commitment by government agencies to effectively implement these policies.

Parents who were aware of the LCA said that they learned about it and other corporal punishment policies in informal settings, such as through listening to the radio, watching television, attending parent-teacher meetings, and participating in activities of non-governmental organizations. In one interview, a mother shared her experience:

> When I attended a parent-teachers meeting, the head of the school told us that corporal punishment was against children's rights. He said we should stop using corporal punishment or where necessary, we should use it reasonably. This surprised me a lot; I asked myself how parents could teach their children good behaviour without using corporal punishment. Personally, I decided not to abide by his explanations. I will keep using corporal punishment to discipline my children. I am sure many other parents did not agree with the head of school, because what he said was against our traditional ways of child rearing.

The fact that many parents relied upon informal sources to obtain information about corporal punishment policies may explain why most were relatively uninformed about the LCA.

Some also asserted understanding that a new paradigm in child rearing was being proposed by the government, which was not healthy for the family or children. They equated the lack of CP with the lack of childcare, contending for instance that children who are left to do whatever they wish, without sufficient parental guidance, were more likely to become disrespectful and irresponsible citizens. One mother commented, "this law will increase chaos in our homes, children will become disrespectful and uncontrollable." Another remarked, "children should always be under the control of their parents. It is through this way that they can learn how to become responsible adult in the future." Further, many parents saw the establishment of the LCA as implying that they were failing to raise their children correctly. This idea annoyed many parents in our study. In relation, they perceived the LCA as being an insult to them and their traditions. As one father commented, "child rearing is a private family matter that should not be interfered by the government. We don't need laws to tell us how to raise our children."

4.3.2 Educators and Educational Policy Makers

In interviews, educational policy makers had higher levels of understanding of corporal punishment laws and policies compared to teachers and parents. Most said that they acquired information about corporal punishment policies by attending seminars and workshops, which were conducted by different governmental agencies and non-governmental organizations. Others said they learned about corporal punishment policies through accessing online sources and by reading books, magazines, and newspapers, which were mostly supplied in their offices by the government through the Ministry of Education. As one educational policy maker put it, "I learned about the Child Act 2009 and other child protection policies, including corporal punishment policy, when I attended a seminar that was organized by a non-governmental organization called Tanzania Child Rights Forum."

All educational policy makers were provided some training about their roles in implementing corporal punishment regulations in schools. The same kind of training was also provided to heads of schools, including the heads of preschools in this study. However, ordinary schoolteachers reported receiving no in-service training or orientation on corporal punishment regulations. Educational policy makers in our study indeed confirmed there has been no formal or systematic arrangement for training schoolteachers related to CP. Here they cited lack of resources, particularly financial resources, as the main hindrance. As one educational policy maker put it:

> We are trying our best to provide education to teachers about alternative punishment, but the truth is we have no fund to reach every school and every teacher. We are running the office under deficit budget, and according to the current economic situation and budgetary allocation, I do not see the possibility of reaching every teacher in the near future.

In interviews, educational policy makers indicated they also received copies of corporal punishment regulations from the Ministry of Education. These copies were distributed to schools to serve as guidelines. However, they also noted that the copies were not sufficient to be distributed to every teacher. This might explain why most teachers indicated that they were not aware of corporal punishment regulations. All heads of school interviewed also said that they never received a copy of corporal punishment regulations from the Office of the School Inspectorate or the Office of the District Education Officer. This discrepancy suggests a lack of effective organization among stakeholders in the implementation of CP regulations.

Most teachers also had limited access to electronic or printed sources of information about corporal punishment policies. Moreover, they were rarely invited to participate in child protection seminars and workshops. Teachers more generally are not involved in the process of school policy formulation. All educational policies are formulated by a department within the Ministry of Education and Vocational Training. Involvement of other key stakeholders, particularly those from the grassroots level, is not given priority. This situation further explains why teachers are ill-informed about child protection policies.

During interviews, some teachers (from both public and private preschools) revealed that they had learned in colleges about "advantages" and "disadvantages" of corporal punishment. The curriculum, in their recollection, did not cover specific policy issues about corporal punishment, however. A more experienced teacher commented in relation, "all that I know about corporal punishment is its advantages and disadvantages. This is what I learned in college. At some point, I heard that corporal punishment is forbidden in schools. I am wondering if these days its disadvantages outweigh its advantages."

Teachers and educational policy makers had contradicting views about corporal punishment policy. Most (75%) educational policy makers indicated that the effective implementation of corporal punishment policy would help promote children's wellbeing and improve school learning. In relation, over half supported government and international initiatives to outlaw the use of corporal punishment in schools. Only a few (35%) expressed that they felt corporal punishment was an effective disciplinary strategy. In contrast, teachers generally viewed corporal punishment policy as an obstacle that would increase unnecessary tension with students. As one teacher said, "I do not support the anti-corporal punishment law because it will lead to poor students' academic performance. It will also make schools unsafe place for children to gain knowledge, discover and develop their potentials." As teachers were not involved in the child protection policy development agenda or policy formulation process, most viewed corporal punishment policy as an external project intended to disrupt their practices.

4.4 Conclusion

This chapter presented findings about the use of corporal punishment in homes and preschool settings in the Dodoma Urban District in Tanzania. The findings revealed that the use of corporal punishment in homes and preschools is influenced by cultural norms and religious beliefs, teacher qualifications, parents' levels of education, past experiences of corporal punishment, psychosocial and demographic factors, and beliefs about the effectiveness of corporal punishment. In general, we found that approval of corporal punishment was low among older parents, teachers with higher levels of professional qualifications, and educated parents. Broadly, however, participants reported that their cultural values and traditions justified the use of corporal punishment. They felt that corporal punishment was an effective way of controlling children's behavior and easy to administer. In schools, teachers felt that corporal punishment helped improve students' academic performance. Parents and teachers asserted that corporal punishment was administered for the purpose of shaping behaviors of the children, and not to harm them.

The educational policy makers we interviewed expressed that they worked to educate teachers about children's rights and the most appropriate uses of corporal punishment in schools. However, they contended that some teachers deliberately ignored guidelines, seeing them as in conflict with their own beliefs. Meanwhile, in the schools we visited, teachers indicated they never received any substantive formal training on alternative discipline strategies. Most teachers we interviewed also argued that the more effective enforcement of corporal punishment policy would not benefit students. According to these teachers, they would be abandoning their role in shaping student behaviour merely to avoid being caught on the wrong side of the law. In their views, this would not only negatively affect student behaviour, but it would also hinder their academic achievement and the general functioning of the school. The next chapter discusses our conclusions and recommendations related to CP with young children in Tanzania.

Chapter 5
Discussion and Conclusion

Abstract Our study sought to examine the use of corporal punishment with young children in Tanzania. This chapter discusses the findings of the study, which were presented in detail in Chapter Four. Here, we examine more broadly in relation to past research the prevalence of corporal punishment with preschool aged children, factors influencing its use by teachers and parents, and the legal and constitutional framework for child rights protection and corporal punishment, globally and in Tanzania. Then we consider the contributions of our study to the research field, and as well as its limitations. Finally, we provide recommendations based on our work, to improve life and society in Tanzania by eliminating corporal punishment, in line with international legal, moral, and rights-based perspectives.

Keywords Tanzania · Corporal punishment · Early childhood education · Preschool education · International perspectives · Children's rights

5.1 Summary of Our Study

Across the world, the use of corporal punishment in homes and schools has attracted much debate (Gershoff, 2002; Gomba, 2015; Khuwaja et al., 2018; Tang, 2006; Wang et al., 2018). Despite the views of some that corporal punishment "works" to eliminate, discourage, or prevent undesired behavior among children, empirical studies consistently indicate that corporal punishment is harmful to children and not educational. Corporal punishment (CP) causes physical discomfort and injuries, distress, and anxiety; it leads to increased aggression and future abusive behavior as it entails the promotion of using physical force rather than other strategies to deal with problems; and in relation, it is strongly associated with a variety of antisocial behaviors, including suicide attempts and drug abuse (Cui et al., 2016; Gershoff, 2002; Hunter et al., 2000; Man et al., 2017; Yang, 2009; Youssef et al., 1998). It is therefore recognized today as a barrier to education globally (UNESCO, 2015).

Morally, corporal punishment entails the loss of dignity of the individual child or person. It is humiliating, disempowering, and can seriously disrupt one's development of capacities to make and act on decisions in line with self-interest. In relation, it puts children in the position to act in accordance with other people's demands that may conflict with their own. While proponents of corporal punishment may argue it is religiously justified, a more systematic consideration of religious teachings suggests that it goes against religious values, of respect for others, dignity, equality, justice, compassion, and non-violence. There is no compelling evidence that CP, as it is practiced in many societies today, is strongly supported by interpretations of the Bible or other religious texts. In relation, major international and regional frameworks such as the United Nations Convention on Rights of the Child (UNCRC) and the African Charter on the Rights and Welfare of the Child (ACRWC) forbid its use, identifying it as harmful and immoral, despite some groups' arguments that it is part of their culture.

Yet proponents of corporal punishment continue to assume that CP is useful in raising responsible children (Gomba, 2015; Maphosa & Shumba, 2010). Many still see it as effective for stopping misbehavior, and as comparably easy and simple to administer (Kuleana, 1997). Scholars have identified various factors which influence the use of corporal punishment. Some are related to characteristics of children, parents, and teachers, while others are family and society related (Dawes et al., 2005; Gershoff, 2002; Hunter et al., 2000; Youssef et al., 1998). However, the applicability of these factors in Tanzanian contexts, particularly with preschool aged children, had not been explored before this study. Where there is past research on corporal punishment in Tanzania indicating that it is common and widespread, it was unknown which factors influenced parents and teachers to use corporal punishment with young children. Our study aimed to fill this gap in the literature, to provide insights and understandings based on parents and teachers' perspectives.

In relation, we found that corporal punishment is commonly used with young children in homes and preschools. More than three-quarters of parents and teachers who participated in our study used corporal punishment to discipline their young children and preschool students. Thus, many young children face corporal punishment at home and preschool. Moreover, we found that many parents and teachers generally support the continued use of CP in child rearing and preschool. In the minds of most parents and teachers, it was difficult if not impossible to differentiate discipline from punishment, and CP was necessary to protect children from harm.

In contrast, the distinction between punishment and discipline is well explained in research. While punishment involves inflicting pain and distress for past behavior, discipline involves "teaching and training the child for desirable future behaviors" (Gershoff, 2002). Relatedly, as discussed by the United Nations Committee on the Rights of the Child, "there is a clear distinction between the use of force motivated by the need to protect a child or others and the use of force to punish"; "As adults, we know for ourselves the difference between a protective physical action and a punitive assault; it is no more difficult to make a distinction in relation to actions involving children" (2006, p. 12).

While our study has focused on experiences of parents and teachers in working with young children, our findings are in many ways comparable to those of previous studies in Tanzania (Feinstein & Mwahombela, 2010; Frankenberg et al., 2010; Hecker et al., 2014; Kuleana, 1997; UNICEF, 2011). Past studies also found that corporal punishment is common and widespread in Tanzania, with children from older age groups. The study by UNICEF (2011) similarly showed that about 75% of children in Tanzania experienced corporal punishment at schools (see also TIE, 2021). The same percent of school-aged children was reported to have experienced corporal punishment in the homes. Hecker and colleagues (2014) revealed that 95% of primary school children in Tanzania had been subjected to corporal punishment in schools, while Kuleana (1997) found that 85% of parents used it at home.

The majority of participants in our study asserted that the use of corporal punishment in child rearing was in line with African tradition and culture. Further, they argued that corporal punishment was part of Tanzanian culture, as it had been used across generations. Thus, many were of the view that the abolition of corporal punishment was against Tanzanian culture. Many were not ready to follow that route, contending that the future of the society would be at stake. Further, participants associated alternative child rearing and disciplinary strategies with the imposition of cultural colonialism or neocolonialism, where western approaches were being imposed to occupy the place of Tanzanian/African attitudes and worldviews. And it was found that in the views of participants, teaching of Christianity and Islam, the two major religions in Tanzania, supported the use of corporal punishment, which also has been found in other studies (Dawes et al., 2005; Gomba, 2015).

There is another side to this story which participants did not mention, however, but which we feel is also significant. In relation to claims about cultural traditions of Tanzania and the neocolonialism of international child rights discourse, we observe that the contemporary intergenerational cultural transmission of CP in Tanzania also has colonial roots. While CP indeed may have been used in precolonial times, it was the German and British colonialists who institutionalized these practices in relation to formal religious, educational, and civil order. These colonialists did not treat Tanzanians of any age according to moral (and religious) values held across societies today (including Tanzania): of human rights and human dignity, equality, and fairness. This, we argue, is another, darker side of the backdrop to the continued use of CP in Tanzania, which we would also like to encourage stakeholders to contend with going forward.

This view also provides an understanding of African cultural as dynamic rather than fixed in time: The laws and standards set in the colonial era are not the essential culture of Tanzania (Jackson, 2013). Over hundreds of years many norms and standards have changed, in Tanzania, in other parts of Africa, and in other societies as well. In this context, it is not necessary to protect or enhance the society to hold onto CP, especially since it is shown to lead not to moral development of the society but also to moral problems, with its facilitating of a cultural of violence, disregard and disrespect for others and their interests and development, and needless experiences of fear and pain, in this case among the most vulnerable members of society.

Many of the factors associated with the use of CP in other studies were also found in our study. These are therefore useful to keep in mind as stakeholders consider how to encourage parents and teachers to stop using CP in early childhood care settings in the future. We found that the use of corporal punishment was more common in larger families than in smaller families. Responses from parents showed that a larger family size is associated with increased parental stress. In this context, since many families in Tanzania and in the Dodoma Region have more than four children (National Bureau of Statistics, 2012), many children in the country are especially vulnerable to corporal punishment. These findings echo those of previous studies (Abolfotouh et al., 2009; Dawes et al., 2005; Day et al., 1998; Dietz, 2000; Flynn, 1994; Xu et al., 2000; Youssef et al., 1998). As McCurdy (2005) found, corporal punishment is often used in large families for the mental and emotional comfort for parents, rather than as a true disciplinary strategy.

We also found that corporal punishment is gender based. Boys are more often subjected to corporal punishment than girls, as culturally, CP is viewed as a part of boys' socialization, to "toughen" them up. Other studies, such as those by Straus (1994), Dawes and colleagues (2005), Gershoff (2002), Day and colleagues (1998) and Tang (2006), revealed similar findings. In addition, young and preschool aged children are more often subject to corporal punishment, as parents and teachers tend to believe that they are incapable of understanding other means of discipline. These findings are consistent with research conducted in India (Hunter et al., 2000), Egypt (Youssef et al., 1998), South Africa (Dawes et al., 2005), the United States (Dietz, 2000), and Hong Kong (Tang, 2006). Relatedly, Youssef and colleagues (1998) observed that young children face corporal punishment because of their more dependent status, and lack of ability for self-defense.

We observed that parents in wealthier families and who were employed used corporal punishment less often than parents with lower socioeconomic status, or who were unemployed. This also echoes previous studies (Dawes et al., 2005; Dietz, 2000; Giles-Sims et al., 1995; Pinderhughes et al., 2000; Straus, 1994; Straus & Stewart, 1999; Tang, 2006; Youssef et al., 1998). As in the studies by Whipple and Richey (1997) and Tang (2006), we found that employed parents spend less time with their children, while unemployed parents were more likely to be stressed and have more conflicts with their children.

In our research, both mothers and fathers reported using corporal punishment, while mothers used it more often than fathers. As noted by Hecker and colleagues (2014), Tanzanian mothers are commonly held as having the primary responsibility to nurture their children in society. When children display inappropriate behaviors, it is seen as causing shame to the family, and to mothers in particular. This is supported by the Swahili proverb, *asiyefunzwa na mamaye hufunzwa na ulimwengu*, which means, "a child who was not taught by their mother would be taught by the world": in other words, "if a child is not taught good manners by their mother, they will have to learn them in the school of hard knocks." To overcome this situation, which is regarded as culturally shameful, mother more often rely on corporal punishment. Our findings here mirror studies by Gershoff (2002), Mahoney and colleagues (2000), Alampay and Jocson (2011), Jocson and colleagues (2012), Dawes and colleagues (2005), Tang (2006), and Baumrind (1996).

Additionally, we observed that younger parents prefer corporal punishment more than older parents, consistent with past studies (Dawes et al., 2005; Dietz, 2000; Straus, 1994; Tang, 2006). Like the current study, previous studies found that younger parents used corporal punishment more than older parents, because they lack parenting experience. According to Tang (2006), the use of corporal punishment in child rearing tends to decrease with the age of parents. As parents grow older, they gain experience and become more tolerant of their children's behaviors. Similarly, we noticed in our study that younger parents had less realistic expectations related to their young children's development and behavior, such as expecting them to sit still for long periods and be silent. As a result, they opted for corporal punishment to try to force their children to reach their less reasonable expectations.

Relatedly, teachers' professional qualifications and parents' educational backgrounds influenced their views about and use of corporal punishment. Parents with lower levels of education were more in favor of corporal punishment than counterparts with higher levels of education. Teachers with less professional training were more likely to use corporal punishment than colleagues with higher professional qualifications. This is particularly noteworthy as teacher education curricula does normally today include information about the negative impacts and illegality of CP, and the use of alternative positive forms of classroom discipline and management. Additionally, recent intervention studies by the Tanzania Institute of Education do indicate the effectiveness of alternative teacher in-service training in Tanzania within a supportive professional environment (TIE, 2021). These findings about the importance of teacher and parent education in relation to CP also echo those identified in studies in different parts of the world, such as South Africa (Maphosa & Shumba, 2010), Uganda (Nagawa, 1998), Kenya (Mwai et al., 2014), Malaysia (Kumaraswamy & Othman, 2011) and Philippines (Manaay, 2013).

Finally, we saw that parents and teachers who experienced corporal punishment during childhood were more likely to use and endorse the strategy. Most parents and teachers who faced corporal punishment in childhood opposed its abolition. And those (few) who were not subjected to corporal punishment supported its abolition. These findings also mirror those of previous studies (Ateah & Durrant, 2005; Chung et al., 2009; Dietz, 2000; Qasem et al., 1998; Sanapo & Nakamura, 2011; Straus, 1994, 2010). There were also some parents and teachers who expressed that they had adverse experiences with corporal punishment. They were more likely to disapprove of its use. As seen in previous studies (Anderson et al., 2002; Clayton, 2011; Nagawa, 1998; Tang, 2006), parents who faced severe and harsh corporal punishment are likely to oppose its use as they associate it with lack of parental care and love.

5.2 Corporal Punishment and the Law

The Tanzanian government enacted the Law of the Child Act (LCA) in 2009 in an official, public effort to implement the UNCRC and the ACRWC, which were ratified by the government in 1991 and 2003, respectively. However, in direct contradiction with the words and the spirit of the UNCRC and ACRWC, the LCA (Article 13) gives parents and guardians legal power to administer corporal punishment to children for disciplinary purposes. Similarly, in Zanzibar, corporal punishment in child rearing and education remains effectively legal. Article 14 of the Zanzibar Children Act

(2011) grants legal power to parents and other guardians to use "reasonable" corporal punishment for the purpose of caring for and educating children.

In schools, the National Education Act No. 25 of 1978 still allows heads of school to use corporal punishment to discipline students, in clear contradiction as well of the UNCRC and ACRWC. The National Education Act also states that teachers should seek permission from the head of school before they administer corporal punishment. However, in practice, this rule is frequently violated. Teachers commonly punish their students without explicit permission from their head; we observed this ourselves, and many parents, teachers, and educational policy makers in our study also confirmed this. CP, even with young children, is simply not considered problematic or illegal to the majority. This is contrary to the legal frameworks of most other countries, such as Sweden, Kenya, South Africa, Zimbabwe, and Uganda, where the use of corporal punishment in school is more clearly legally prohibited (Busienei, 2012; Dawes et al., 2005; Gomba, 2015; Lansford et al., 2010).

In our study, we found that general social, cultural, and legal acceptance of corporal punishment was one of the reasons for its common use. This suggests that corporal punishment will continue to be common until the government more fully enacts law to forbid it. Various studies have established that the law is an important tool that can bring attitude change against corporal punishment (Straus, 1994). In particular, experience from Sweden, the first country to outlaw the use of corporal punishment in all childcare settings, showed that the introduction of law and its effective implementation, including public education and related teacher preservice and in-service training about alternative parenting and disciplinary strategies, led to the loss of public support for CP (Bussmann, 2009).

However, many parents who participated in our study expressed that they did not support the establishment of national law that would effectively prevent corporal punishment. Participants insisted in this context that corporal punishment was used for disciplinary purposes only. Therefore, they said that children's discipline was a family matter that should not attract government attention. Further, they indicated that they felt that the abolition of corporal punishment would not be healthy for children, despite compelling evidence to the contrary. Thus, many parents and teachers felt that it was their right to punish children.

Some asserted that the government should prevent "severe" corporal punishment. However, it is difficult in practical and situational contexts to effectively draw a line between severe and mild corporal punishment. This view is supported by Dawes and colleagues (2005), who found that many incidents of physical child abuse start as a "normal," socially accepted punishment. But during execution, parents who fail to control their anger or related emotions are inclined to become more severe and ultimately to abuse their children. This is another important reason why law should bar all kinds of corporal punishment in all settings.

On the other hand, we found that the majority of parents were not aware of the existence of the Law of Child Act. Similarly, many teachers were not aware of regulations that guide and restrict the administration of corporal punishment in schools. This is due in part to the top-down nature of policy formulation. Parents and teachers as stakeholders in children's rights protection are not involved in the process of children's rights policy formulation. During policy implementation, parents and teachers thus fail to abide by requirements of the policy and laws because of conflicting beliefs about and understandings of the law. Therefore, most parents expressed that corporal punishment policy was an unnecessary government intervention in family matters. Similarly, many teachers had the view that the effective implementation of corporal punishment regulations was likely to cause more harm than good. In relation, few parents or teachers reported that they had significant exposure to alternative means of discipline and punishment for children. However, the small minority of participants who were aware of alternative methods and strategies tended to favor them, and rely less upon CP.

5.3 Contributions and Recommendations

Although our study was conducted on a small scale, it was the first to specifically explore the use of corporal punishment with young children in homes and preschools in Tanzania. This topic has not attracted much attention thus far, because of its normalcy in society. Thus, by researching this internationally controversial topic in a society where the use of corporal punishment is not only accepted and cherished, but also customarily encouraged and praised by government leaders, we hope to open a more informed public debate about the legitimacy of corporal punishment, particularly in early childhood care and in preschool education. Additionally, this study opens the doors for further research on this important but neglected topic. In relation, we list our major recommendations for future research and for future practice (policy and education) in Tanzania.

5.3.1 Recommendations for Future Research

1. Given its continued normalcy in society, there is insufficient contemporary research on corporal punishment and other forms of violence against children in Tanzania. Studies on corporal punishment and other topics related to violence against children can help further raise public awareness about the harmful impacts of corporal punishment and related violent punishments. This, in turn, can help stakeholders to identify better practices and strategies for raising and teaching children.
2. More specifically, a moral, religious, and rights-based view has not been customarily employed in past research, but arguments in this domain are significant for understanding the continued use of CP in Tanzania, as well as pathways for persuading key stakeholders to discontinue and help prevent its use in the future. People use and support CP for what they hold to be moral, religious, and cultural reasons, with positive intentions. Moral, religious, and cultural reasons

can also be supplied to discourage CP. Intervention and action research studies in this domain, such as the recent research by the Tanzania Institute of Education (TZI, 2021), are thus worthwhile in this domain.

3. Our study focused on young and preschool-aged children (aged 0–6 years old). Older children and adolescents were not involved. Available evidence in Tanzania shows that these groups also experience corporal punishment at home and in school (Feinstein & Mwahombela, 2010; Hecker et al., 2014; Kaltenbach et al, 2018; Kuleana, 1997). However, a more comprehensive contemporary study that includes a national sample of children across age groups should be undertaken to gain a clearer, more explicitly comparative picture.

4. Our study focused on corporal punishment, which we understand is set within a broader spectrum of violence against children. Other forms of violence against children, such as sexual violence, psychological violence, and neglect and abuse were not explicitly or systematically examined here, and they have not been the focus of past research in Tanzania. Future research should examine these aspects to develop a broader picture of the situation of violence against children in Tanzania.

5. The findings of our study do not focus on corporal punishment administered by members of the extended family, such as aunts, uncles, and other relatives. Studies in India (Hunter et al., 2000) and Egypt (Youssef et al., 1998) reveal that children are punished not only by parents, but also by other relatives. This situation is likely to occur in Tanzania. Future research could be framed in such a way that all of those involved in the child rearing process could be involved as research participants.

5.3.2 Recommendations for Future Practice

1. The government should effectively implement legislation and policy to prohibit CP in homes and schools in Tanzania in alignment with moral, religious, and evidence-based arguments against the practice and international and regional frameworks to which the government has indicated support (that is, the UNCRC and the ACRWC).

   (a) This would involve, firstly, scrapping and replacing the 1930 British colonial Corporal Punishment Ordinance still in place today, the National Education Act No. 25 of 1978, the Zanzibar Education Act of 1982, and the LCA and ZCA, all of which legally permit the continued use of corporal punishment.

   (b) Secondly, new legislation should explicitly ban the use of all forms of corporal punishment in childcare and education, with no exceptions.

   (c) New legislation should include provision and support, including material and human resources (that is, funds for dedicated staff and print and online materials), for widespread public education and more systematic and comprehensive preservice and in-service teacher training, in home languages, on the harms, inefficacy, and illegality of CP, as well as special further continuous educational support for parents, families, and educators. Part and parcel of this education is learning about other practices for caring for, raising, and educating children across developmental phases, and intersecting information sharing about typical behaviors and reasonable expectations for children in different phases of development, as well as the significance of early childhood development and the use of alternative parenting and educational strategies to facilitate children's cognitive as well as emotional, social, and moral development, and the positive, non-violent development of the community at large. It should be emphasized that CP and other forms of violent punishment harm child development and social development by encouraging a culture of fear in schools and a culture of violence in society.

(d) Relatedly, efforts should be made to clarify that banning CP does not imply a "lack of control" and need not facilitate "moral decay" or westernization. Rather, control and assurance of child and community wellbeing can more effectively be secured using alternative childcare and educational strategies, apart from CP.

(e) Finally, legislation must entail a system of accountability, wherein it is specified which governmental or other institutions are responsible for ensuring the effective implementation of anti-CP policy and law and providing for related educational and other measures and necessary resourcing (funding).

2. As discussed here, key stakeholders have been left out of relevant educational policy development processes in the past, including parents and families, religious leaders, youth, and ordinary school educators. In deliberating and deciding upon the details of procedures around (among other things) education about and accountability regarding CP law, such stakeholders should be consulted with in a democratic and culturally appropriate manner. Without significant grassroots support, understanding, and input, laws and policies are unlikely to meet with wide public approval to be successfully implemented. This makes consultation with grassroots and other ground-level stakeholders crucial for effective policy implementation in relation to CP, among other issues (see also Jackson, 2013; Kahembe & Jackson, 2020).

3. Religious leaders in Tanzania should be systematically enabled to coordinate and collaborate with religious leaders elsewhere in Africa and worldwide in order to develop a broader view of CP, as not particularly aligned with religious or other relevant moral or spiritual teachings, and as intersecting with the colonial legacies of the region and the world, thus developing a view of CP as more than simply a religiously informed or African "traditional" practice (Churches' Network for Non-violence, 2015).

4. All people, but especially young people, should be systematically introduced to a child rights view that recognizes CP and other violence against children

(at home and at school) as harmful, wrong, and illegal, through education and related social institutions, across the country.

(a) In relation, teachers and other community leaders should be equipped to manage and encourage youth and adult reporting of cases of harm and violence, through a safe and secure social network to ensure the development of children in Tanzania in the future.

(b) This entails systematic supports across governmental levels in society, to ensure that children and community members who report on cases of harm and violence against children (among others, such as those with special needs, women, and other vulnerable members of society) can remain safe in their community. If children, teachers, or other community members are fearful of negative repercussions due to reporting, given an environment where CP and other forms of violence are still basically accepted within a culture that permits such violence, then mechanisms for true implementation and necessary accountability will remain challenging if not impossible to access.

5. Finally, improving the quality of education as a whole is foundational to the success of future efforts to eliminate CP schools in Tanzania. Teacher and school leader preservice and in-service education should be enhanced more generally, along with the working conditions of educators, including providing for reasonable salaries and benefits, and improving of school environment and infrastructure. In relation, class sizes should be restricted. As many educators and educational policy makers commented in our study, managing a large class size is quite difficult and stressful for educators; many teachers feel that alternative disciplinary techniques are easier to use in smaller classes. While the Tanzanian government aims to reach smaller class sizes than what has been the norm in the past, more should be done to ensure that smaller and more reasonable class sizes can become standard in the future. In sum, more societal resources should go into education, to ensure it is effective and beneficial for students and society in myriad aspects. Improving school quality will improve teaching and learning and reduce perceived interests in using CP for managing school discipline. Investing in education is necessary to value and recognize the importance of the future development of society more generally.

5.4 Limitations

Our study is not without limitations. As it was conducted in the Dodoma Urban District, our findings might not be generalized to all of Tanzanian society due to sociocultural and economic variations. Tanzania has more than 120 ethnic groups, with diverse cultural and historical backgrounds (Malipula, 2014). Additionally, most findings were based on participants' self-report, so there could be under-reporting or over-reporting of information (Juvonen et al., 2000). Some might not have been comfortable enough to disclose openly and frankly important information related to their attitudes and practices. This could be due to the sensitive nature of the topic, or because of the "culture of silence," where children's discipline issues are considered private matters. This last point reflected the view of one of our interviewees, who pointedly asked during the study, "do you want to teach us how to discipline our children?" Also, instruments for data collection, such as interviews and question-naires, were translated from English to Kiswahili, and in some cases to other home languages of participants, to ease understanding. Then again, participants' responses were translated to English for presentation here. In this process sometimes the precise and intended meaning can be changed or lost.

5.5 Conclusion

Our study reported on the prevalence and factors influencing the use of corporal punishment of young children in homes and preschool settings in Tanzania. Infor-mation about the nature and effectiveness of existing legal frameworks for child protection and corporal punishment in Tanzania was also presented. Our findings showed that corporal punishment is common and widespread. Young children are normally subjected to corporal punishment by parents, teachers, and other adult members of the community. The use of corporal punishment with young children is influenced by multiple and overlapping factors. Some of these relate to children's characteristics, while others relate to parents and teachers' characteristics. Other factors relate to the culture and laws of the country.

Most participants in our study saw corporal punishment as necessary to instill discipline and obedience. The move to ban its use in homes and preschools was rejected by most teachers and parents. Meanwhile, existing legal frameworks for child protection and corporal punishment do not address the intention to ban its use in homes, schools, and other childcare settings. The lack of involvement of parents and teachers in policy formulation leads to their holding a negative impression about the objectives of such policies.

This study contributes to the literature on corporal punishment globally by unveiling attitudes and identifying factors influencing the use of corporal punish-ment young children in Tanzania. It also provides policy implications for children's rights protection. However, most importantly, we hope that this work opens the door for greater society-wide reflection in Tanzania about the nature and use of CP across the lifespan, given the significance of early childhood development and education for a person's opportunities in life, and the particularly common use of CP with the youngest, most vulnerable members of society.

Upholding children's rights is not about coddling or spoiling children. Within a cultural context wherein children are recognized as valued members of society, eliminating CP does not lead to moral or societal decay, or children being harmfully "out of control." It is not in the educational or other best interest of children (or any other persons) to face negative physical or emotional repercussions because of others' disapproval of their behavior. In the case of young children, play and activity are key to their development. CP does not "teach" children moral lessons in this context. Instead, thwarting natural processes of child development in an absolute, violent way harms children's emotional and cognitive wellbeing and hinders their education, despite the desires of parents and teachers for well-mannered and quiet children.

A healthy, compassionate, just, and spiritually and morally aligned community works to protect the wellbeing and interests of all its members, including its most vulnerable members. Working from the ground up, development of the person and the community are interrupted by cultures of corporal punishment and other forms of unnecessary, degrading community-based violence. The measure of a healthy, moral, and just society is in how it treats its weakest members. Protecting children from violence, including corporal punishment, is the responsibility of all.

References

Abolfotouh, M., El-Bourgy, M., Seif El-Din, A. & Mehanna, A. (2009). Corporal punishment: Mother's disciplinary behavior and child's psychological profile in Alexandria, Egypt. *Journal of Forensic Nursing, 5*(1), 5–17.

Alampay, L. P., & Jocson, M. R. M. (2011). Attributions and attitudes of mothers and fathers in the Philippines. *Parenting: Science and Practice, 11*, 163–176.

Anderson, S., Murray, L., & Brownlie, J. (2002). *Disciplining children: Research with parents in Scotland*. Scottish Executive Central Research Unit.

Ateah, C., & Durrant, J. (2005). Maternal use of physical punishment in response to child misbehavior: Implications for child abuse prevention. *Child Abuse and Neglect, 29*(2), 169–185.

Baumrind, D. (1996). The discipline controversy revisited. *Family Relations, 45*, 405–415.

Busienei, A. J. (2012). Alternative methods to corporal punishment and their efficacy. *Journal of Emerging Trends in Educational Research and Policy Studies, 3*(2), 155–161.

Bussmann, K. D. (2009). *The effect of banning corporal punishment in Europe: A five-nation comparison*. Martin-Luther-University.

Chung, E., Mathew, L., Rothkopf, A., Elo, I., Coyne, J., & Culhane, J. (2009). Parenting attitudes and infant spanking: The influence of childhood experiences. *American Academy of Pediatrics, 124*(2), 287–286.

The Churches' Network for Non-violence (CNNV). (2015). *Ending corporal punishment of children—A handbook for working with religious communities*. The Global Initiative to End All Corporal Punishment of Children.

Clayton, C. (2011). Contemporary British Chinese parenting: Beyond cultural values. *Childhoods Today, 5*(1), 1–25.

Cui, N., Xue, J., Cynthia, A., Connollya, L., & Liu, J. (2016). Does the gender of parent or child matter in child maltreatment in China? *Child Abuse & Neglect, 54*, 1–9.

Dawes, A., Kropiwnicki, Z., Kafaar, Z., & Richter, L. (2005). *Corporal punishment of children: A South African national survey*. Human Science Research Council.

Day, R. D., Peterson, G. W., & McCracken, C. (1998). Predicting spanking of younger and older children by mothers and fathers. *Journal of Marriage and the Family, 60*, 79–94.

Dietz, T. L. (2000). Disciplining children: Characteristics associated with the use of corporal punishment. *Child Abuse & Neglect, 24*(12), 1529–1542.

Feinstein, S., & Mwahombela, L. (2010). Corporal punishment in Tanzania's schools. *International Review of Education., 56*, 399–410.

Flynn, C. P. (1994). Regional differences in attitudes towards corporal punishment. *Journal of Marriage and the Family, 56*, 314–324.

Frankenberg, S. J., Holmqvist, R., & Rubenson, B. (2010). The care of corporal punishment: Conceptions of early childhood discipline strategies among parents and grandparents in a poor and urban area in Tanzania. *Childhood, 17*(4), 455–469.

Gershoff, E. T. (2002). Corporal punishment by parents and associated child behaviors and experiences: A meta-analytic and theoretical review. *Psychological Bulletin, 128*, 539–579.

Giles-Sims, J., Straus, M. A., & Sugarman, D. (1995). Child, maternal and family characteristics associated with spanking. *Family Relations, 44*(2), 170–176.

Gomba, C. (2015). Corporal punishment is a necessary evil: Parents' perceptions on the use of corporal punishment in school. *The International Journal of Research in Teacher Education, 6*(3), 59–71.

Hecker, T., Hermenau, K., Isele, D., & Elbert, T. (2014). Corporal punishment and children's externalizing problems: A cross sectional study of Tanzanian primary school aged children. *Child Abuse & Neglect, 38*, 884–892.

Hunter, W., Jain, D., Sadowski, L., & Sanhueza, A. (2000). Risk factors for severe child discipline practices in rural India. *Journal of Pediatric Psychology, 25*(6), 435–447.

Jackson, L. (2013). They don't *not* want babies: Globalizing philosophy of education and the social imaginary of international development. In C. Mayo (Ed.), *Philosophy of education 2013* (pp. 353–361). Philosophy of Education Society.

Jocson, R. M., Alampay, L. P., & Lansford, J. E. (2012). Predicting Filipino mothers' and fathers' reported use of corporal punishment from education, authoritarian attitudes, and endorsement of corporal punishment. *International Journal of Behavioral Development, 36*(2), 137–145.

Juvonen, J., Nishina, A., & Graham, S. (2000). Self-views versus peer perceptions of victim status among early adolescents. In J. Juvoven & S. Graham (Eds.), *Peer harassment in schools: The plight of the vulnerable and victimized* (pp. 105–124). Guilford.

Kahembe, J., & Jackson, L. (2020). *Educational assessment in Tanzania: A sociocultural perspective*. Springer.

Kaltenbach, E., Hermenau, K., Nkuba, M., Goessmann, K., & Hecker, T. (2018). Improving interaction competencies with children—A pilot feasibility study to reduce corporal punishment. *Journal of Aggression, Maltreatment and Trauma, 27*(1), 35–53.

Khuwaja, H., Karmaliani, R., McFarlane, J., Somani, R., Gulzar, S., & Ali, T. S. (2018). The intersection of school corporal punishment and associated factors: Baseline results from a randomized controlled trial in Pakistan. *PLoS ONE, 13*(10), 20–30.

Kuleana. (1997). *Study on corporal punishment in primary schools in Mara region*. Kuleana Centre for Children's Rights.

Kumaraswamy, N., & Othman, A. (2011). Corporal punishment study: A case in Malaysia. *Psychology, 2*, 24–28.

Lansford, J. E., Alampay, L., Al-Hassan, S., Bacchini, D., Bombi, A., Bornstein, M. H., & Zelli, A. (2010). Corporal punishment of children in nine countries as a function of child gender and parent gender. *International Journal of Pediatrics*, 1–12.

Mahoney, A., Donnelly, W. O., Lewis, T., & Maynard, C. (2000). Mother and father self-reports of corporal punishment and severe physical aggression toward clinic-referred youth. *Journal of Clinical Child Psychology, 29*, 266–281.

Malipula, M. (2014). Depoliticized ethnicity in Tanzania: A structural and historical narrative. *Africa Focus, 27*(2), 49–70.

Man, X., Richard, P., Barth, B., Lia, Y., & Wang, Z. (2017). Exploring the new child protection system in Mainland China: How does it work? *Children and Youth Services Review, 76*, 196–202.

Manaay, S. M. (2013). *Discipline in the Philippine context: Factors affecting parents' use of corporal punishment* (Unpublished PhD Thesis). The Chicago School of Professional Psychology

Maphosa, C., & Shumba, A. (2010). Educators' disciplinary capabilities after the banning of corporal punishment in South African schools. *South African Journal of Education, 30*, 387–399.

McCurdy, K. (2005). The influence of support and stress on maternal attitudes. *Child Abuse & Neglect, 29*, 251–268.

Mwai, B. K., Kimengi, I. N., & Kipsoi, E. J. (2014). Perceptions of teachers on the ban of corporal punishment in pre-primary institutions in Kenya. *World Journal of Education, 4*(6), 90–100.

Nagawa, P. J. (1998). *Corporal punishment and behavior of primary school pupils of Kampala District* (Unpublished Masters Dissertation). Maker ere University, Uganda.

National Bureau of Statistics (NBS), (2012). *Tanzania national population census report*. Government Press.

Pinderhughes, E. E., Dodge, K. A., Bates, J., Pettit, G., & Zelli, A. (2000). Discipline responses: Influences of parents' socioeconomic status, ethnicity, beliefs about parenting, stress, and cognitive-emotional processes. *Journal of Family Psychology, 14*(3), 380–400.

Qasem, F., Mustafa, A., Kazem, N., & Shah, N. (1998). Attitudes of Kuwait parents toward physical punishment of children. *Child Abuse and Neglect, 22*(12), 1189–1202.

Sanapo, M. S., & Nakamura, Y. (2011). Gender and physical punishment: The Filipino children's experience. *Child Abuse Review, 20*, 39–56.

Straus, M. A. (1994). *Beating the devil out of them: Corporal punishment in American families*. Lexington Books.

Straus, M. A. (2010). Prevalence, societal causes, and trends in corporal punishment by parents in world perspective. *Law and Contemporary Problems, 73*, 1–30.

Straus, M. A., & Stewart, J. H. (1999). Corporal punishment by American parents: National data on prevalence, chronicity, severity and duration in relation to child and family characteristics. *Clinical Child and Family Psychology Review, 2*(2), 55–70.

Tang, C. S. (2006). Corporal punishment and physical maltreatment against children: A community study on Chinese parents in Hong Kong. *Child Abuse & Neglect, 30*, 893–907.

The Tanzania Institute of Education & UNESCO. (2021). *Connect with respect: Curriculum for improving learning environment through building skills for respectful and non-violent relationship in Tanzanian schools*. Tanzania Institute of Education.

United Nations Committee on the Rights of the Child. (2006). *General comment No. 8: The right of the child to protection from corporal punishment and other cruel or degrading forms of punishment*. United Nations.

UNESCO. (2015). *School-related gender-based violence is preventing the achievement of quality education for all*. UNESCO.

UNICEF. (2011). *Violence against children in Tanzania: Findings from a national survey 2009*. UNICEF Tanzania.

Wang, F., Wang, M., & Xing, X. (2018). Attitudes mediate the intergenerational transmission of corporal punishment in China. *Child Abuse & Neglect, 76*, 34–43.

Whipple, E., & Richey, C. (1997). Crossing the line from physical discipline to child abuse: How much is too much? *Child Abuse and Neglect, 21*(5), 431–444.

Xu, X., Tung, Y., & Dunaway, R. G. (2000). Cultural, human, and social capital as determinants of corporal punishment: Toward an integrated theoretical model. *Journal of Interpersonal Violence, 15*, 603–630.

Yang, S. (2009). Cane of love: Parental attitudes towards corporal punishment in Korea. *British Journal of Social Work, 39*, 1540–1555.

Youssef, R. M., Attia, M. S., & Kamel, M. I. (1998). Children experiencing violence II: Prevalence and determinants of corporal punishment in schools. *Child Abuse & Neglect, 22*(10), 975–985.

The manufacturer's authorised representative in the EU is Springer
Nature Customer Service Centre GmbH, Europaplatz 3, 69115 Heidelberg,
Germany. If you have any concerns regarding our products, please
contact ProductSafety@springernature.com

Printed and bound by CPI Group (UK) Ltd, Croydon, CR0 4YY

29/04/2026

02099458-0017